EDUCATION AND SOCIOLOGY

Emile Durkheim

EDUCATION AND SOCIOLOGY

TRANSLATED, AND WITH AN INTRODUCTION, BY
SHERWOOD D. FOX

FOREWORD BY TALCOTT PARSONS

The Free Press, New York
Collier-Macmillan Limited, London

LC
191
.D772

Library of Congress Catalog Card Number: 55-11002

printing number
3   4   5   6   7   8   9   10

CONTENTS

FOREWORD

by Talcott Parsons

One of the most important services performed by The Free Press in its brief existence has been to make available to the professional public, through reprint and translation, a whole series of the "classics" of modern social science, especially sociology, which otherwise would be likely to have been seen by only a few rather recondite scholars. The present translation belongs in this already extended series. Its special importance lies in the fact that it brings to those social scientists who have not read most of Durkheim's writings in French, an aspect of his work which is relatively little known to American readers—judging by secondary references to Durkheim—but which figured very prominently in it and in his position in France, namely, his work in the field of education. Durkheim's professorship at the Sorbonne was a professorship of sociology *and* education, and he lectured in this field for many years. This work undoubtedly had a great deal of influence on the shaping of his general sociological thinking, as well as being an important contribution to the field itself. Dr. Fox and The Free Press are hence to be congratulated in making some of it available to us.*

---

* The other most important work of Durkheim in this field is *L'Education morale*, a course of lectures given at the Sorbonne in 1902-03, but only published posthumously in 1925 (edited by Paul Fauconnet, Paris: F. Alcan).

As Dr. Fox remarks in his Introduction to the English Translation, in spite of the fact that work done a long generation ago and in another country has many features which seem remote to contemporary Americans, at the same time, many of the things in this set of essays seem surprisingly up to date. Indeed, there is a sense in which in a good many ways we have only recently caught up with the level of both sociological analysis and shrewd observation which Durkheim commanded. There is one major theme of this work on which I would like to make a few comments.

Durkheim, for understandable reasons, came to be known in the social science professions as either the great opponent of psychological interpretations and emphases in general, or as the proponent of an "unsound" psychological doctrine, namely, that of the *conscience collective*, or as it was most generally known in the English-speaking world, the "group mind." Polemical attitudes toward the formulae in which Durkheim's views were expressed have tended to inhibit more penetrating exploration of the actual structure of his thought, and hence to obscure the very positive contributions which Durkheim made precisely to the interrelations of sociology and psychology.

The formulae to which I refer were largely determined by a specific intellectual tradition in which Durkheim worked and by the polemical situation in which he found himself, especially vis-à-vis Tarde. In his critique of Tarde and, for instance, in the critique of psychological interpretations of suicide rates, he was concerned above all to assert the independent significance of the sociological level of analysis as against tendencies to psychological "reductionism." It is only rather recently, if now, that this can be taken for granted even in sociology, and it is by no means securely established in the psychological profession.

8

But there is another side to Durkheim's work in this respect, a side which perhaps first clearly emerged in his seminal conception of *anomie* as first fully developed in *Le suicide*. Here already was clearly implied the *internalization* of socio-cultural norms, since he interpreted anomic suicide as resulting from disorganization of the relation of the personality to its internalized moral culture. The theme was considerably farther developed in later work, and culminated in certain parts of *The Elementary Forms of the Religious Life*, notably perhaps in the famous formula, "society exists exclusively within the minds of individuals." If the special technical sense of the term society in this passage be taken into account, it is clear from this and other evidence that Durkheim must be accorded, with Freud, the credit for what undoubtedly is one of the most fundamental of all *psychological* discoveries, namely, that of the fact of internalization of culture as part of the structure of the personality itself, not simply as providing an "environment" within which the personality or the organism functioned.

This is to say that Durkheim, by virtue of the path along which his sociological analysis took him, was led deep into psychological theory and made extremely important contributions to it. He cannot fairly be considered simply as the sociologist who opposed psychology, nor as the psychologist of the "unsound group mind," but was the contributor of more than one highly creative idea in psychology which is in the forefront of the development of that field today. Indeed, the relations of the two disciplines are such that he could not, in my opinion, have carried his analysis of social systems as far as he did without becoming deeply involved in the psychology of personality.

The biographical evidence seems to show that his work in education played a critical part in leading him to the insights which made this articulation of psychology and sociology possible. He started in his early theorizing with the twin criteria of "exteriority and constraint" as the hallmarks of social facts. Constraint in the earlier period was interpreted as either the pressure of the non-social environment or external coercion by others. It was in his writings on education that he first stated that there was another possible interpretation, namely, that constraint should be by "moral authority," and this clearly meant through the internalization of norms.

This is the setting in which I think it is relevant to understand the greatest importance of Durkheim's work on education not only for sociology, but for social science more generally. The reader will find many rich insights and suggestions as to the way in which what we now call the process of socialization takes place. His work in this field is a monument to the thesis that no satisfactory theory of education, as of many other social phenomena, can be developed without the contribution at strategically important places of several disciplines, in this case notably *both* sociology and psychology. Durkheim set a model for the general framework of that collaboration which to this day is one of the best we have.

INTRODUCTION TO
THE ENGLISH TRANSLATION

by Sherwood D. Fox

Sociologists in the mid-twentieth century, drawing as they do upon the cumulative efforts of several generations of predecessors, may sometimes be unmindful of the importance of the pioneering work of Emile Durkheim. He was one of three Europeans, contemporaries, to whom American sociology owes much, particularly among certain of its practitioners; the other two, of course, were Vilfredo Pareto and Max Weber. During the lifetime of these men, their work had little influence upon sociology in the United States, and it is only in the past twenty years or so that American sociologists have begun to discover its fruitfulness. Although *Les formes élémentaires de la vie religieuse* (1912) was translated in England in 1915, it was not until 1933 that *De la division du travail social* (1893) became available in English, in 1938, *Les règles de la méthode sociologique* (1895), and, in 1950, *Le suicide* (1897). It is these four major works by which Durkheim is best known to Americans.* However, there are a substantial number of American sociologists who consider his work of such importance that

---

* The Free Press now publishes all of these.

they welcome the making available, in English, of this collection of papers on education.

For the new generation of sociologists, notably those who have been developing functional analysis, Durkheim stands as a significant precursor, as a source of many productive suggestions. There are those who, at least half-seriously, regard sociology as some fifteen to twenty years old; this view neglects, of course, the long history of attempts to observe, understand and predict human social action. Still, the scientific period of this history is relatively short, and the point here is that the work of Durkheim represents a landmark in the more recent period of the development of sociology as a science.

It is not the purpose of this introduction to attempt to assess the reasons for the belated appreciation of the significance of Durkheim's contribution to sociology, or to undertake an intensive analysis of his thought or his background. However, one is struck by the fact that much of the work that has been translated in this volume sounds as fresh, as lively, as current, as though it had been written yesterday instead of when it was, some forty to fifty years ago. At point after point, Durkheim has set down propositions that have become part of the universe of discourse of sociology. The very phrases used, the very types of relationships indicated, emphasize the magnitude of his achievement.

On the other hand, the reader may detect a certain quaint or archaic quality in some of the phraseology used, which has been left in translation, as well as in some of the conceptual material. Discrimination is obviously necessary. To illustrate certain problems of translation, we may take the term "pedagogy." This word was much in use at the turn of the century and before, not only among educators, but also among other specialists who had occasion to deal with education, such as psychologists, both in Europe and in the United States; today, we rarely use it. Another term is "conscience," which has been variously interpreted. Much of the early, relatively unsophisticated American interpretation of Durkheim may be attributed to misinterpretation of this concept. Related to this is "individual," which has been a controversial concept in American sociology and psychology. Clearly, Durkheim did not mean the concrete personality by this, as most American sociologists do not today. Far from operating with notions of a "collective unconscious" or "collective consciousness," Durkheim stressed the exteriority and constraint of social facts, as a category of phenomena *sui generis*, different and distinct from "individual facts." These distinctions drawn by Durkheim, so little understood at an earlier period, are now an integral feature of current sociological theory.

Other peculiarities of wording are seen in such words as "reflection." Again, as in the case of pedagogy, past usage has changed; where we now use "think," Durkheim, as well as Americans of the same period, used "reflect." Or, in the case of "moral," it should be remembered that the sense in which this word is used is its derivation from "mores," rather than the American sense of ethics.

In addition to the crossing of the language barrier, there is the further fact, already noted, that these papers were written forty to fifty years ago, in France. The broad social setting and academic milieu in France at the turn of the century were quite different from the contemporary American scene in general, and specifically with respect to the educational system and the organization of sociology. It is useful, then, to keep in mind such differences in time and place. The taking for granted of public education in France in Durkheim's period, the controversy over the place of the church and of the state in education, the insistence on a *lay* morality—these are some of the differentiating features of a sociocultural system different from ours, and it is against this background that these papers are to be understood.

Further insight into the intellectual climatc of the time may be gained through the enumeration of a few of Durkheim's contemporaries, in sociology and psychology, in Europe and in the United States. Having worked with Breuer (1842-1925) on hysteria, Freud (1856-1939) went to Paris to study with Charcot (1825-1893), who had developed his famous clinic for diseases of the nervous system; this early work of Freud took place in the 1880's, and includes a visit to Nancy where Liébault and Bernheim were also working on hysteria. In the 1890's, Janet (1859-1947) was director of Charcot's clinic, continuing studies in hysteria and hypnosis.

In the United States, the 1890's marked the beginnings of a period of relatively mature work in psychology, particularly in its relevance to education. Among the psychologists active around the turn of the century were Dewey (1859-1952), G. Stanley Hall (1846-1924), Morton Prince (1854-1929), G. H. Mead (1863-1931), Boris Sidis (1867-1923), and E. L. Thorndike (1874-1949). William James (1842-1910), in his *Talks to Teachers* (lectures delivered from 1892 on), observed the great "fermentation" among teachers for over a decade, with respect to the purposes and methods of education; he also noted the advances in the study of psychology, in relation to the help that teachers expected of it. Up to that time, there was no systematic theory of teaching, and there were many expressions of an urgent need for a "science of pedagogics." A point of view congenial with Durkheim's was expressed by James in his

14

observation that science lays down limits within which practice may proceed, and that psychology cannot lead to the formulation of programs.

In sociology, some representative Europeans were Spencer (1820-1903), Tarde (1843-1904), Pareto (1848-1923), Toennies (1855-1936), Simmel (1858-1918), and Weber (1864-1920). Representative figures in the United States at this time include Sumner (1840-1910), Ward (1841-1913), Small (1854-1926), Giddings (1855-1931), Cooley (1864-1020), and Ross (1866-1951).

Several characteristics of French sociology, which apply also to Durkheim himself, are worth noting at this point. First, the general point of view of sociology, in France, was rather widely diffused among many types of scholars, making its influence felt in such disciplines as history, geography, and others. Second, and this point is especially relevant for Durkheim, the inadequacies of the psychology that he had at his disposal are apparent. Third, the orientation of French sociology to the work of "social reconstruction" is significant —at the time when sociology in the United States showed this characteristic even more sharply (cf. recruitment of sociologists from ministers and sons of immigrants). It is not accidental that Durkheim was interested in moral conclusions, that he wanted his work to have practical results. But he very carefully distinguished between scientific analysis and the application of the findings of science—a distinction not so well understood in the United States at that time.

This last point may be illuminated by consideration of the analytical distinction between the two roles of scientist and citizen, occupied by the same individual. Although he was interested in bringing sociological findings to bear upon practical problems, Durkheim explicitly tried to think and speak as a scientist in his attempt to analyze and understand education in its relationships to the social system. Even to-day, in the United States, there are still those who do not grasp this simple distinction, but who seem to believe that since one and the same person plays the two roles of scientist and citizen, the roles themselves cannot be distinguished.

Over fifty years ago, Durkheim was doing pioneer work in establishing modern sociological methodology, as distinguished from the "study of society" or "science of customs." His apparently polemic attitude toward psychology may be understood in terms of the low level of development of psychology at the time, as well as in terms of the degree to which psychology, even today, has been able to cope with some of the problems that he raised. In his conception of pedagogy, he tried to outline the respective relevancies of sociology and psychology for education, with a lively sense of the limitations of each of these emerging disciplines. The interpenetration of sociology and psychology in the United States today has gone far, by contrast, at least in part because of the advances made in each, and because of definite steps in the direction of an emerging theory of human social action, to which each of these sciences contributes.

As a sociologist, Durkheim was very much interested in education, for he gave courses in pedagogy throughout his career. This concern hardly appears in his major works, as known to English-speaking sociologists, but can be seen in the present collection of articles, in *L'Education morale,* and in various uncollected articles. The value of the papers translated here is twofold, since the material presented is relevant not only for educators, but also for sociologists. It is precisely the application of the sociological approach to education that makes these analyses useful to those interested in education from a practical point of view, as well as to sociologists. Durkheim treats systems of education in terms of their relationships to the total social systems in which they occur; this leading principle of his method is one of the basic features of much contemporary sociological inquiry, and the details of the analyses prove the fruitfulness of this mode of attack, in the clarification of the functions of education. There can be no doubt that this kind of insight is of the highest value for educators today, particularly from the point of view of providing perspective on their activities and making them aware of the context of their actions.

In addition to this general significance of these papers on education, there may be cited a series of themes, problems for further investigation, insights, and provocative statements, all of which can fruitfully be re-examined and considered by contemporary sociologists. Among these manifold and varied lines of thought, four may be singled out for special attention, under the following headings: (1) sociology of science and knowledge, (2) the historical approach, (3) sociology of personality, and (4) social science and social practice. These are not listed in order of importance, and each will be discussed in turn; the fourth point will be reserved for last, since Durkheim himself was much concerned with it, and because the present writer is also engaged in this area of inquiry.

(1) Those who are interested in the sociology of knowledge will find, throughout these pages, further food for thought (in addition to what is available in *The Elementary Forms of the Religious Life,* and in various other works of followers of Durkheim) on a number of problems. For example, Durkheim shows how science has not always existed, and that it is not to be found everywhere; it arises in re-

sponse to certain needs that develop at a given stage of development in a given sociocultural system. At this point, certain critics of functional analysis, and/or those insufficiently acquainted with functionalism in sociology, are likely to question the category of social needs; therefore, a brief comment, from the point of view of functional sociology, is in order. Although he is a precursor of current functional analysis, Durkheim never formulated it in anything like the terms developed by Parsons and Merton, Malinowski or Radcliffe-Brown. However, a concept of societal needs is basic to functional sociology, and perhaps the readiest clarification may be provided by the distinction between two sets of needs, which, nevertheless, have important interrelations: those of a social system as a going concern, and those of individual members of the social system. In order to continue to exist, any social system must contain provisions for such fundamental desiderata as maintenance of personnel, production and distribution of goods and services, internal order, and others; these are societal needs, or functional prerequisites of a social system, and they are universal. Thus, our social system requires engineers; but no specific member of this social system has to become an engineer; and the relation between societal needs and needs of members is seen in the fact that *some* members become motivated, and have the opportunity, to become engineers. Durkheim saw this more or less clearly, when he pointed out how certain specific sets of actions or beliefs develop from the interaction of the universal societal needs and the derived needs stemming from the operation of a specific culture. This is the context of his discussion when he speaks of education as answering social needs; he did not reify any particular set of actions, but, rather, stressed "institutional compatibility" among the constituent elements of a going social system.

18

To return to Durkheim's contributions to the sociology of knowledge: he stresses the collective nature of scientific activity, and the creative force of society itself in the production of patterns of thought. Fifty years ago, he stated clearly the crucial quality of culture for the distinctive nature of human social interaction. He understood, too, the differentiation of function of the intellectual under specified social conditions. The inverse relationship between tradition and thought is set forth plainly, against a background of comparative cultures. If these notions are familiar, today, this cannot be said of Durkheim's time. He was one of the great innovators whose ideas have spread so widely as to become almost the common sense of a later generation.

(2) A second theme centers around the uses of history in sociological inquiry. Weber and Mosca, to name only two contemporaries (working, respectively, in economic history and in political science), also looked to history along similar lines. In his critical discussion of the widespread notion of the existence of a single, ideal form of education, Durkheim supports his argument by showing empirical variations in systems of education in space and time, citing Athens, Rome, the Middle Ages, and the Renaissance. Education, for him, cannot be understood apart from its historical context, either at a given moment or over time. This same sensitivity to history also illuminates the discussions of the origins and development of science and other forms of knowledge and social action. In this connection, he shows how pedagogy itself does not appear until a relatively advanced period in history, only when this kind of thought is called for by social conditions.

As pedagogical reflection becomes part of the ongoing educational process, it must address itself to history in order to be able to understand the social institution, education, in its historical continuity, says Durkheim. Tracing given trends through history to their origins contributes to fuller knowledge of their causes and operation. History, as a source of comparative cases, provides an indispensable means of putting into context a given social phenomenon, in this case, education. From the point of view of practice, too, Durkheim observes that one cannot build anew, but only on the basis of existing institutions, which have a history. Historical and comparative method is essential for the determination of the changing ends of education, and for the understanding of trends; it is history alone that can penetrate beneath the surface of a social phenomenon.

(3) With respect to the sociology of personality, Durkheim also appears modern, as may be seen in his general approach to human nature and personality. In his day, relations between sociology and psychology were less than cordial (as contrasted with the situation in the United States today, at least among some of the best practitioners in the two fields), as each maintained a kind of imperialistic attitude toward the other. Thus, Durkheim had to improvise, at certain points, with great success in some cases. Certainly, his conception of the plastic nature of the newly-born infant fits current theories, as well as his notions on the creative force of society and culture in creating a "new being" of the child through socialization; as he put it, "Man is man, in fact, only because he lives in society." This formulation stresses our contemporary emphasis on interaction situations and actual experiences as fundamental formative forces in the development of personality. In this connection, further, the cumulative effect of human culture is also noted. Both Cooley and Durkheim, in the same period, saw that the individual and society are not opposed, but, rather, imply each

20

other; that it is life in society that makes of an individual a truly human being.

It may not be too much to say that there are, in Durkheim's work on education, the germs of the fundamental approach of what are now called "Culture and Personality" studies, for he repeatedly pointed out the relationships between the requirements of a given sociocultural system and the social personalities of its members. He may have been pushed in this direction by his reactions to the individualistic conceptions of personality offered by the psychologists of his time, in his attempts to order his observations. It is the society, he says, that gives form to any innate predispositions, adding to and changing them in the process.

(4) The general problem of the relationships between social science and social practice is the fourth of the lines of thought abstracted from these articles on education. In addition to his other interests, Durkheim taught courses in pedagogy, always treating it from the sociological point of view, which he regarded as eminently suited to this subject; he was in the fortunate position of being able to address directly the future teachers of France. He could give them, thus, at least some notion of the problems with which they would be dealing, concerning which he could contribute sociological analysis. Although we cannot measure the efficacy of this teaching, most of what he has to say about the relationships between a system of education and the society in which it operates sounds authentic to the sociologist of today.

As has been mentioned, although Durkheim thought of himself primarily as a scientist, he was also aware of his role as a citizen and wanted his scientific work to find practical applications. This side of Durkheim appears with especial clarity in his treatment of education, as seen in his numerous statements to the effect that knowledge is the fundamental prerequisite for efficacious action. He looks to psychology, for example, for knowledge of how consciousness operates, in order that educational practice may be effective in shaping the "consciences" of children. And he offers sociology as the means for discovering what the ends of education should be. This division of labor between sociology and psychology is consistently maintained by Durkheim: sociology can determine ends, and psychology, means, of educational practice.

Intensely aware of the deep-seated changes going on in his country and in other industrial societies, Durkheim felt that never was sociology more needed by educators, in their attempt to understand what societal needs education was to meet, first, and then to refashion the educational system in accordance with those needs. Indicating the complexity of secondary education in particular, he said that more and more thinking was needed, and that the teachers themselves had to be guided in pedagogical reflection so that they might participate more effectively in the work of reconstruction and reorganization. In this process, historical study is indispensable for understanding of the educational system, so that those engaged in the reconstruction might better be able to build upon the existent structure. And one of the means by which this work was to be performed was through Durkheim's own lectures, in which he tried to show the future teachers how science can serve as a guide to human behavior; through scientific inquiry, knowledge is acquired, which is then applied in practice.

These thoughts of Durkheim may be amplified in a few final remarks on the relations between social science and social practice. Durkheim was fully aware of the limitations

22

of the sociology and psychology of his time; although there have been very outstanding advances in both these fields since then, we may well retain a measure of his humility in the face of our inability to solve many of the problems of our science, to speak for sociology alone. Over and above such strictures, however, sociology can probably contribute more to social practice than is being asked of it. Durkheim took the position that his work was intended to have practical applications. Although he thought and worked as a sociologist, developing sociological analyses of the problems with which he dealt, he viewed such analyses as leading to conclusions that might be applied in social practice. Ultimately, since science is a social, collective activity, it must yield some "value" to the society which makes it possible—in the modern world, if we take the example of the physical and biological sciences, practical applicability has been a significant criterion of value. This same criterion applies equally well to the social sciences in general, and to sociology in particular.

One of the chief obstacles to establishing sociological theory is the difficulty of testing hypotheses through the application of tentative conclusions. A suggested line of activity is an increase of interaction between sociologists and the personnel of action agencies, explicitly oriented toward systematic exploration of the mutual relevance of social science and social practice. This type of interaction is suggested because of the increased possibilities, in it, along two related lines: improvements in the "public relations" of sociology, hand in hand with possibilities for building a more reliable science. These two go together, it would seem, in much the same way as the use of hospital facilities increased as the facilities themselves improved; that is, when hospitals were dangerous, there was public resistance to using them; and as the techniques of medicine were improved through the application of science, so that hospitals became safer, people began to lose their realistic fear of them. Similarly, as sociologists get into action situations, action personnel can learn from them, and discover what sociology can contribute to social action; at the same time, the sociologists can learn from the action personnel, and discover hitherto unsuspected errors of omission or commission the correction of which can lead to advancement of theory.

A concluding comment will necessarily be brief, and intended primarily as a point of departure for further investigation. Although we have much to learn in the general area of relations between social science and social practice, it is necessary to make explicit another element of action, namely, power. Any social system has a power structure: a set of relations between those who make decisions, and those who carry out the decisions. Some actions are performed according to the application of science; other actions are performed according to the operation of the power structure. In the latter process, to be sure, science may be applied at points where means to ends are sought—but it is important to see that science does not provide norms for social practice, or, that there are other considerations than science (contrary to the hopefulness of positivists) that enter into the determination of social practice. Although these considerations are neither original nor unknown, it is useful to mention them, here, as part of the context of the relations between social science and social practice, in the hope that this growing area of inquiry may profit from the co-operative research fostered by such questions.

Since Paul Fauconnet, at the end of his introduction to the French edition, has provided a description of the dates and places where the four articles that constitute the chapters of this book were originally published, the reader is referred to page 57 for this information. The French text contains seven footnotes, four of which (two in Fauconnet's Introduction, and two in Chapter III) have been omitted on the grounds that they contribute nothing to the reader's understanding, for they refer to works which are out of date and/or inaccessible to the contemporary American reader. The other three footnotes (one at the end of Fauconnet's Introduction, and two at the beginning of Chapter IV) have been retained for their informative value. Since Durkheim refers to many individuals, in his discussions of pedagogy, whose names in this connection may be unfamiliar to the reader outside the field of education, I have added an Appendix of pedagogical references.

There remains only the pleasant task of acknowledging the debts which always accompany the preparation of a book.

Talcott Parsons is responsible for the original suggestion that it would be a service to sociologists and to educators to make this work available in English; for this idea, for his encouragement and advice, and for the stimulation that he has always offered, I am sincerely grateful.

The onerous task of checking the manuscript for accuracy in the rendering of the French was ably performed by Gisèle Ganz; for this assistance, and for her many useful suggestions, I am most appreciative.

For assistance in the preparation of the Index, I should like to thank my friend and former student, Terence K. Hopkins, who has enlivened the teaching role of a sociologist.

Finally, I welcome the opportunity to express a widely shared and lively feeling of appreciation to Jeremiah Kaplan who, as editor of The Free Press, has the well deserved gratitude of social scientists for his long list of significant publications in this field of scholarship.

And to Marcia, Jane and Jonathan, this small expression of my great indebtedness.

Westport, Connecticut
February, 1956

INTRODUCTION TO THE ORIGINAL EDITION

DURKHEIM'S PEDAGOGICAL WORK

by Paul Fauconnet

Durkheim taught pedagogy all his life, at the same time that he taught sociology. In the Faculty of Letters at Bordeaux, from 1887 to 1902, he always gave a weekly one-hour lecture on pedagogy. His audience consisted mainly of primary school teachers. At the Sorbonne, it was in the chair of "Science of Education" that in 1902 he substituted for, and in 1906 replaced, Ferdinand Buisson. Until his death, he reserved for pedagogy at least a third, and often two-thirds, of his teaching: public lectures, conferences for primary school teachers, lectures for the students of the Ecole Normale Supérieure. This pedagogical work is almost entirely unpublished. No doubt, none of those who heard him grasped its whole scope. We should like to present it here in abridged form.

I

Durkheim divided neither his time nor his thinking into two distinct, unrelated categories. He approaches education through its being a social fact: his theory of education is an essential element of his sociology. "As a sociologist," he says, "it is above all as a sociologist that I shall speak to you of education. Moreover, in proceeding in this way, far from handling phenomena with a biased frame of reference, I am, on the contrary, convinced that there is no method better suited to demonstrating their true nature." Education is an eminently social thing.

Observation proves it. First, in each society, there are as many special types of education as there are different social milieux. And, even in egalitarian societies such as ours, which tend to eliminate unjust differences, education varies, and must necessarily vary, from one occupation to another. No doubt, all these special types of education have a common base. But this common education varies from one society to another. Each society forms its own ideal of man. It is this ideal "which is the focus of education." For each society, education is "the means by which it secures, in the children, the essential conditions of its own existence." Thus, "each type of people has its own education, that is appropriate for it, and that can serve to define it, just as its moral, political and religious organization." Observation of facts leads, then, to the following definition: "Education is the influence exercised by adult generations on those that are not yet ready for social life. Its object is to arouse and to develop in the child a certain number of physical, intellectual and moral states that are demanded of him by both the political society as a whole and the special milieux for which he is specifically destined." More briefly, "education is a socialization . . . of the young generation."

But why is this necessarily so? It is "because in each of us, it may be said, there exist two beings which, while inseparable except by abstraction, remain distinct. One is made up of all the mental states that apply only to ourselves and to the events of our personal lives: it is what might be called the individual being. The other is a system of ideas, sentiments and tendencies which express in us, not our personality, but the group or different groups of which we are part; these are religious beliefs, moral beliefs and practices, national or professional traditions, collective opinions of every kind. Their totality forms the social being. To constitute this being in each of us is the end of education." Without civilization, man would be only an animal. It is through co-operation and through social tradition that man becomes man. Systems of morality, languages, religions, sciences are collective works, social things. Now, it is by morality that man forms in himself the will that overcomes desire; it is language that raises him above pure sensation; it is in religions, first, then in sciences, that are elaborated the cardinal notions of which the distinctively human intelligence is made. "This social being is not given, fully formed, in the primitive constitution of man. . . . It is society itself which, to the degree that it is firmly established, has drawn from within itself those great moral forces. . . . The child, on entering life, brings to it only his nature as an individual. Society finds itself, then, with each new generation, faced with a *tabula rasa*, very nearly, on which it must build anew. To the egoistic and asocial being that has just been born, it must, as rapidly as possible, add another, capable of leading a moral and social life. Such is the work of education." Heredity transmits the instinctive mechanisms that assure organic life and, among animals that live in societies, a rather simple social life. But it is not sufficient to transmit the aptitudes that social life presupposes of man, aptitudes too complex to be able "to take the form of organic predispositions." The transmission of the specific attributes that distinguish man is effected through a social channel, as they are social: education.

To anyone trained to regard things from this point of

view, this sociological conception of the nature and role of education is quite clear from the evidence. Durkheim calls it a fundamental axiom. Let us say, more exactly, a truth of experience. We see clearly, when we think historically, that education in Sparta is the Lacedaemonian civilization making Spartans for the Lacedaemonian city; that Athenian education, in the time of Pericles, is the Athenian civilization making men modeled on the ideal type of man as Athens conceives him in this period, for the Athenian city and, at the same time, for humanity, as Athens conceives of it in relation to herself. We need only ponder on the future to understand how historians will interpret French education in the twentieth century: even in its most audaciously idealistic and humanitarian efforts, it is a product of French civilization; it consists of transmitting it; in short, it seeks to make men, modeled on the ideal type of man that this civilization implies, to make men for France, and also for humanity, as France defines it in relation to herself.

However, this truism has generally been unrecognized, especially during the past centuries. Philosophers and pedagogues agree that education is an eminently individual thing. "For Kant," writes Durkheim, "for Kant as for Mill, for Herbart as for Spencer, the object of education would be above all to realize, in each individual, but carrying them to their highest possible point of perfection, the attributes distinctive of the human species in general." But this agreement is not a guarantee of truth. For we know that classical philosophy has almost always failed to consider the real man of a given time and place, the only one that is observable, in favor of speculating on a universal human nature, the arbitrary product of an unsystematic abstraction from a very limited number of human samples. It is generally admitted, today, that its abstract character has vitiated, in large measure, the political speculation of the eighteenth century, for example: overly individualistic, too detached from history, it often sets up laws for an artificial man, independent of any definite social milieu. The progress made in the nineteenth century by the political sciences, under the influence of history and the philosophies inspired by history, progress toward which all the moral sciences are oriented at the turn of the century, the philosophy of education must accomplish in its turn.

Education is a social thing; that is to say, it puts the child in contact with a given society, and not with society in general. If this proposition is true, it does not simply lead to speculative reflection on education, it must make its influence felt on educational activity itself. In practice, this influence is indisputable; as a matter of principle, it is often disputed. Let us examine some of the types of opposition aroused by Durkheim's proposition.

First, one hears the protestation that may be called universalistic or humanistic: that sociology encourages a narrow nationalism, indeed, sacrifices the interests of humanity to those of the State, or, even worse, to the interests of a political regime. During the war, German education was often contrasted with Latin education, the former purely national and all for the benefit of the State, and the latter liberal and humanistic. No doubt, it has been said, education rears the child for Country, but *also* for Humanity. In short, in various ways, there is established an opposition between these terms: social education, human education, society and humanity. Now, Durkheim's thought is considerably above objections of this type. He never meant, as an educator, to make national ends prevail over human ends. To say that education is a social thing is not to formulate a program of education; it is to state a fact. Durkheim holds this fact to be true everywhere, whatever the prevailing trend may be. Cosmopolitanism is no less social than nationalism. There are civilizations that require the educator to place Country above all, and others that require him to subordinate national ends to human ends, or, better, to harmonize them. The universalistic ideal is tied up with a synthesizing civilization that tends to combine all others. Moreover, in the contemporary world, each nation has its own cosmopolitanism, its own humanism, in which its genius is expressed. What is, indeed, for us, Frenchmen of the twentieth century, the relative value of duties to Humanity and duties to Country; how do they come into conflict; how can they be reconciled? Noble and difficult questions, these, that the sociologist does not resolve in the interest of nationalism, in defining education as he does. When he deals with these problems, he is not committed to a given stand. To recognize that education is actually a social thing does not at all prejudice the manner in which one will analyze the moral forces which influence the educator in one direction or another.

The same answer will serve for the individualistic objections. Durkheim defines education as socialization of the child. But then, some think, what becomes of the value of the human person, the initiative, responsibility, perfectibility of the individual. People are so accustomed to opposing society to the individual, that every theory that makes frequent use of the word society seems to sacrifice the individual. Here, again, they are mistaken. If any man has been an individual, a person, in every sense that this term implies of creative originality and resistance to collective influences, it is Durkheim. And his moral theory corresponds so well to his own character, that one would not be proposing a paradox by giving to this theory the name of individualism. His

32

first work, *The Division of Labor in Society,* offers a whole philosophy of history in which the genesis, the differentiation, and the freeing of the individual appear as the dominant trait of the progress of civilization, the exaltation of the human person, as its actual limit. And this philosophy of history results in a moral rule: be a distinct personality. How, then, could such a theory see in education any process of depersonalization? If the making of a person is actually the end of education, and if to educate is to socialize, let us conclude, then, according to Durkheim, that it is possible to individualize while socializing. This is indeed his thought. We can discuss the way in which he conceives education for individuality. But his definition of education is that of a thinker who does not for a moment fail to recognize, or underestimate, the role or the value of the individual. And it is necessary to point out to sociologists that it is in his analysis of education that they will see best the foundation of Durkheim's thought on the relationships of society and the individual, and on the role of the elite in social progress.

In the name of the ideal, finally, Durkheim's realism is opposed. He will be reproached for abasing reason and discouraging effort, as though he were the systematic apologist for what is and remained indifferent to what *ought to be.* To understand how, on the contrary, this sociological realism appeared to him suitable for guiding action, let us look at his ideas on pedagogy.

II

All Durkheim's teaching answers a profound need of his mind, which is the essential requirement of the scientific mind itself. Durkheim feels a real revulsion for arbitrary constructions, for programs of action that express only the desires of their authors. He needs to reflect on a *datum,* on an observable reality, on what he calls a *thing.* To consider social facts as things, is the first rule of his method. When he talked about moral matters, he first presented facts, things; and his very mode of expression showed that, although it was a matter of spiritual, not material, things, he was not content to analyze concepts, but that he grasped, demonstrated, dealt with realities. Education is a thing, or, in other words, a fact. Indeed, education is found in all societies. In conformance with tradition, usages, explicit or implicit rules, in a given institutional framework, with its own mechanisms, under the influence of collective ideas and sentiments, in France in the twentieth century, educators educate, children are educated. All this can be described, analyzed, explained. The notion of a science of education is, then, a perfectly clear idea. Its unique role is to know, to understand what is. It is confused neither with the effective activity of the educator, nor even with pedagogy, which is concerned with guiding this activity. Education is its object: we mean, by that, not that it works toward the same ends as education, but, on the contrary, that it assumes them, inasmuch as it studies education.

Durkheim does not at all question that this science is, in large measure, psychological. Psychology alone, based on biology, broadened by pathology, makes possible the understanding of why the human child needs education, in what respects he differs from the adult, how his senses, his memory, his faculties of association and attention, his imagination, his character, his will, are formed and evolve. The psychology of the child, related to that of adult man, rounded out by the psychology of the educator himself, is one of the ways in which science can approach the study of education. This idea is universally accepted.

But psychology is only one of the two possible approaches. Whoever follows it exclusively exposes himself to approaching the fact, education, through only one of its two aspects. For psychology is obviously inadequate, with respect to saying not what the child is, who is educated, his manner of assimilating it and reacting to it, but the very nature of the civilization that education transmits and of the mechanisms that it employs to transmit it. France of the twentieth century has four levels of education: primary, secondary, higher, and technical, the relations among which are not at all what they are in Germany, in England, or in the United States. Her secondary education rests on French, the classical languages, living languages, history, sciences; around 1600, it was based exclusively on Latin and Greek; in the Middle Ages, on dialectics. Our education gives a place to inductive and experimental method; that of the United States, a much larger place; medieval and humanistic education was exclusively based on books. Now, it is clear that scholastic institutions, disciplines, methods, are social facts. Books are themselves social facts; the cult of the book, and the decline of this cult, depend on social causes. One does not see how psychology could understand it. The physical, moral and intellectual education provided by a society at a given moment in its history, is manifestly within the province of sociology. To study education scientifically, as a fact given to observation, sociology must collaborate with psychology. In one of its two aspects, the science of education is a sociological science. It is from this point of view that Durkheim approached it.

In doing this, he opened up a new path, impelled by the internal logic of his own thought, the precursor, and not imitator, of theories today very much in vogue, which his own surpasses in clarity and fruitfulness. Germany has created the term "Social Pedagogy," the United States, the term "Educational Sociology," which show, certainly, the same tendency. But these terms still often cover very different things; for example, on the one hand, a more or less vague orientation toward the sociological study of education, as Durkheim conceives it, and, on the other hand, a system of education that is preoccupied more specifically with preparing man for social life, forming the citizen: "Citizenship Education," as Kerschensteiner calls it. The American idea of "Educational Sociology" applies, in a confused way, to the sociological study of education and, at the same time, to the introduction of sociology into classes, as a subject matter. The science of education defined by Durkheim is sociological, in a much clearer sense of the term.

As for what he means by "Pedagogy," it is neither the educational activity itself, nor the speculative science of education. It is the systematic reaction of the second on the first, the work of reflection that seeks, in the results of psychology and of sociology, principles for the conduct or for the reform of education. Thus conceived, pedagogy can be idealist without becoming utopian.

That a goodly number of eminent pedagogues have yielded to the spirit of system, assigning to education an unattainable or arbitrarily chosen end and proposing artificial procedures, not only does Durkheim not deny, but, better than anyone else, he provides a warning against their example. Sociology is here fighting its usual enemy: in all fields, in morality, in politics, even in political economy, the scientific study of institutions has been preceded by an essentially *factitious* philosophy, which claimed to formulate prescriptions to assure to individuals or to peoples the maximum happiness, without first adequately taking into account the conditions of their existence. Nothing is more contrary to the intellectual habits of the sociologist than to specify, *a priori,* how the child must be raised, disregarding the education that is really given him. Scholastic frameworks, curricula, methods, traditions, usages, tendencies, ideas, ideals of the teachers—these are facts, concerning which sociology tries to discover why they are what they are, rather than presuming, first, to change them. If French education is largely traditional, little disposed to adopt the technical forms of newly contrived methods; if it stresses mainly the faculties of intuition, tact and initiative of the teachers; if it respects the free development of the child; even if it results, for the majority, not in the systematic influence of the teachers, but in the diffuse and nonvoluntary influence of the milieu, it is a fact which has its causes and which corresponds, roughly, to the conditions of existence of French society. Pedagogy inspired by sociology does not, then, risk becoming the apologist for an adventitious *system,* or of urging a *mechanization* of the child, which would run counter to his spontaneous development. Thus fall the objections of eminent thinkers, who insist upon opposing Education to Pedagogy, as if to reflect upon the influence that is exerted were necessarily to distort this influence.

But this is not to say that scientific reflection is practically sterile, and that realism is the characteristic of the conservative mind, which lazily accepts everything that is. To understand, in order to predict and to control, Auguste Comte said of positive science. Indeed, the better one knows the nature of things, the better can one use such knowledge efficaciously. The educator is obliged, for example, to guide the attention of the child. No one will deny that he will direct it better if he knows its nature more exactly. Psychology, then, offers practical applications, from which pedagogy formulates the rules for education. In the same way, the sociological science of education can offer practical applications. Of what does the secularization of morality consist?

What are its causes? Whence come the resistances that it arouses? What difficulties has moral education to overcome, when it becomes dissociated from religious education? A manifestly social problem, this, a real one for contemporary societies: how can anyone doubt that its disinterested study can lead to the formulation of pedagogical rules, by which the French teacher of the twentieth century might profitably be inspired in his educational practice? Social crises, social conflicts have causes: this does not mean that we may not seek solutions for them. Institutions are neither absolutely plastic nor absolutely resistant to any deliberate modification. To adapt them wisely to their respective roles, to adapt them to one another and each of them to the civilization of which they are part, provides a fine field of action for a rational *politics,* and, with respect to educational institutions, for a rational *pedagogy,* neither conservative nor revolutionary, efficacious within the limits within which the deliberate action of man can be efficacious.

In this way realism and idealism can be reconciled. Ideals are realities. In fact, to take an example, contemporary France has an intellectual ideal; it conceives of an ideal type of intelligence that it presents to the child. But this ideal is complex and confused. Each of the publicists, who claim to express it, generally shows only one of its aspects, one of its elements: elements of origin, of age and, so to speak, of different orientation, some of them harmonious with certain social tendencies, others, with different or opposite tendencies. It is not impossible to treat this complex ideal as a thing, that is to say, to analyze its constituent elements, to determine their genesis, their causes and the needs to which they correspond. But this study, at first quite disinterested, is the best preparation for the *choice* that a rational will can propose to make among the various con-

ceivable programs of instruction, among the rules to follow
for the implementation of the chosen program. One might
repeat the same thing, *mutatis mutandis*, of moral education, and of questions of detail as well as of more general
problems. In short, the public, legislators, administrators,
parents, teachers constantly have choices to make, whether
it is a matter of basic reform of institutions or of making
them function from day to day. Now, they are dealing with
a resistant material that does not let itself be handled arbitrarily: social milieu, institutions, usages, traditions, collective tendencies. Pedagogy, to the degree that it depends on
sociology, is the rational preparation for these choices.

Durkheim attached the highest importance, not only as
a scientist, but also as a citizen, to this rationalistic conception of action. Hostile to reformist agitation, which disturbs
without improving, above all to negative reforms, which
destroy without replacing, he had, however, a feeling and a
taste for action. But, in order that action be fruitful, he
wanted it to rest upon what is possible, limited, definite,
given in the social conditions in which it is applied. His
pedagogical teaching, addressing itself to educators, always
had an immediately practical character. Absorbed in his
other work, he did not have the time to devote to purely
speculative inquiries on education. In his courses, subjects
were treated according to the scientific method just defined.
But the choice of subjects was dictated by the practical difficulties that the public school teacher in contemporary
France encounters, and Durkheim comes to pedagogical
conclusions.

III

Durkheim left a completed manuscript of a course of
eighteen lectures on "Moral Education in the Primary

School." This is its general outline. The first lecture is an introduction on lay morality. Here Durkheim defines the moral task which, in contemporary France, is incumbent upon the teacher: his job is to give a lay, rationalist, moral education. This secularization of morality is called for by the whole historical development. But it is difficult. Religion and morality have been so intimately related, in the history of civilization, that their necessary dissociation could not be a simple operation. If one is content to empty morality of all religious content, one mutilates it. For religion expresses, in its own way, in a symbolic language, certain truths. These truths must not be allowed to be lost along with the symbols that are eliminated; they must be recovered and projected on the level of secular thought. Rationalist systems, especially nonmetaphysical systems, have presented a greatly oversimplified picture of morality. In becoming sociological, moral analysis can give a rational foundation, neither religious nor metaphysical, to a morality as complex as, even richer in certain respects than, traditional religious morality, and can go back again to the sources from which the most vigorous moral forces spring.

The lectures that follow are grouped in two quite distinct parts, and this plan illustrates what we have said about the contribution made to pedagogy by sociology on the one hand and psychology on the other. The first part studies morality in itself, that is to say, the moral civilization that education transmits to the child; it is a sociological analysis. The second studies the nature of the child who is to assimilate this morality; here psychology is in the foreground.

The eight lectures which Durkheim devoted to the analysis of morality are the best of what he left on this subject, since his death interrupted him at the time when he was writing up, for publication, the outlines of his "Morality."

They are related to the pages which appeared in the *Bulletin of the French Philosophical Society* on "The Determination of the Moral Fact." Here he does not treat specific duties, but the general characteristics of morality. It is the equivalent, for him, of what the philosophers call theoretic morality. But the method that he applies throws new light on the subject.

It is readily apparent how sociology can study what the family, the state, property, contract actually are. But, when it is a matter of Good and of Duty, it seems that one is dealing with pure concepts, not with institutions, and that a method of abstract analysis is imposed, here, for lack of appropriate observation. This is the point of view from which Durkheim approaches his subject. The role of moral education is, no doubt, to initiate the child into various duties, to create in him, one by one, particular virtues. But its role is also to develop in him the general aptitude for morality, the fundamental dispositions that are at the root of moral life, to constitute in him the moral agent, ready to exercise the initiative which is the condition of progress. What, indeed, in contemporary French society, are the elements of the moral temperament, the realization of which is the end toward which general moral education should tend? These elements can be described, their nature and their role can be understood. And it is, finally, this description that forms the content of the moralities called theoretic. Each philosopher defines, in his own way, these fundamental elements. But he constructs, rather than describes. We can do the same thing, taking as our object, not our own personal ideal, but the ideal which is actually that of our civilization. Thus the study of moral education allows us to grasp, in the facts, the realities to which correspond the very abstract concepts that the philosophers deal with. It puts the science of customs in a position to observe what morality is, in its most general characteristics, because, in education, we perceive morality at the moment when it is being transmitted, at the moment when, therefore, it is distinguished most clearly from individual consciences, in the complexity of which it is usually enveloped.

Durkheim reduces to three these fundamental elements of our morality. They are the spirit of discipline, the spirit of abnegation, and the spirit of autonomy. Let us indicate, by way of example, what plan Durkheim follows in the analysis of the first element. The spirit of discipline is, at the same time, the feeling and the taste for regularity, the feeling and the taste for the limitation of desires, the respect for rules, which imposes on the individual inhibition of impulses and effort. Why does social life demand regularity, limitation, and effort? Then, how is it that the individual finally accepts these difficult requirements as the conditions of his own happiness? To answer these questions is to say what the function of discipline is. How is society qualified to impose discipline and, in particular, to awaken in the individual the sentiment of respect due to the authority of a categorical imperative which appears as transcendent? To answer this question is to treat the nature of discipline and its rational foundation. Why, finally, is it that rules can and must be conceived as independent of any religious, or even metaphysical, symbolism? In what respect does this secularization of discipline modify the very content of the idea of discipline, what it requires and what it allows? Here we are relating the nature and function of discipline no longer to the conditions of civilization in general, but to the particular conditions of existence of the civilization in which we live. And we investigate whether our spirit of discipline, ours, as Frenchmen, is indeed all that it should be, or if it is not pathologically weakened, and how education, while preserving its integrity, can improve our national morality.

A parallel analysis applies to the spirit of abnegation. What is it, of what use is it, from the point of view of the society as well as the point of view of the individual? What are the ends to which we, Frenchmen of the twentieth century, ought to devote ourselves? What is the hierarchy of these ends, and whence come, and how can be reconciled, their partial antagonisms? The same questions apply to the spirit of autonomy. The analysis of this last element is especially fruitful, because this question concerns one of the most recent traits of morality, the most characteristic trait of the secular and rationalistic morality of our democratic societies.

These summary indications suffice to mark out one of the principal points of superiority of the method followed by Durkheim. He succeeds in showing the whole complexity, the whole richness of moral life, a richness made up of opposites which can never be more than partially resolved in an harmonious synthesis, a richness such that no individual, however outstanding he may be, can ever hope to carry within himself, in their highest degree of development, all those elements and thus to realize wholly, in himself alone, the entire morality. Durkheim was personally, as Kant had been, above all a man of will and of discipline. It is the Kantian aspect of morality that he sees first and most clearly. There are those who have wanted to make constraint the only influence, according to him, that society exercised on the individual. His actual theory is infinitely more comprehensive, and there is perhaps no moral philosophy that is so to the same degree. He has demonstrated, for example, that moral forces which constrain and even go against the animal nature of man also exercise a strong fascination for man, and that it is to these two aspects of the moral fact that the two notions of duty and of good correspond. And he has shown that two distinct moral activities are oriented to these two poles, of which neither is foreign to the true moral agent, but which, according to whether one or the other prevails, distinguish moral agents into two different types, the man of sentiment, of enthusiasm, in whom the aptitude for giving himself is dominant, and the man of will, colder and more austere, in whom the sense of rule is dominant. Eudemonism and hedonism themselves have their place in the moral life: there must, Durkheim once said, be Epicureans. Thus disparate, even contradictory elements are combined in the richness of the moral civilization, a richness that the abstract analysis of the philosophers is generally doomed to impoverish because, for example, it wants to deduce the idea of the good from that of duty, to reconcile the concepts of obligation and of autonomy, and thus to reduce a very complicated reality to the logical play of some simple ideas.

The nine lectures that form the second part of the course touch upon the pedagogical problem proper. We have just enumerated and defined the elements of morality that it is up to us to constitute in the child. How does the nature of the child lend itself to receiving it; what resources, what means, but also what obstacles, does the educator meet there? The titles of the lectures suffice to indicate the line of thought: first, *discipline and psychology of the child, school discipline, school reward and punishment;* then, *altruism in the child* and *the influence of the school milieu on the formation of the social sense:* finally, the general influence of instruction in sciences, letters, history, morality itself, and also esthetic culture, on *the formation of the spirit of autonomy.*

44

Autonomy is the attitude of a will that accepts rules, because it recognizes that they are rationally based. It presupposes the free but methodical application of the intelligence to the examination of the ready-made rules that the child first receives from the society in which he is growing up, but which, far from accepting passively, he must gradually learn to give new life to, to reconcile, to purify of their decayed elements, to reform, in order to adapt them to the changing conditions of existence of the society of which he is becoming an active member. It is science, says Durkheim, that confers autonomy. It alone teaches us how to recognize what is grounded in the nature of things—physical nature as well as moral nature—what is ineluctable, what is modifiable, what is normal, what are, then, the limits of effective action to improve nature, physical and moral. All education, from this point of view, has a moral end, in the cosmological sciences, but especially instruction on man himself, through history and through sociology. And it is thus that the complete moral *education* today calls for a *teaching* of morality: two things that Durkheim distinguishes clearly, although the second serves to achieve the first. It seems indispensable, to him, even in primary school, that the master teach the child about the situations in which he is called upon to live: family, corporation, nation, the civilized community that tends to include the whole of humanity; how they were formed and transformed; what effect they have on the individual and what role he plays in them. Of the course that he gave several times on this "Moral Education in the Primary School," we have only rough drafts or plans of lectures. Here Durkheim shows teachers how it is possible to interpret, to put within the comprehension of children's intelligence, the results of what he called the "physiology of law and customs." It is the popularization of the science of

customs to which he devoted, elsewhere, the major part of
his works and of his courses.

IV

"Intellectual Education in the Primary School" is the
subject of a course completely written out, and also parallel
to the one on moral education and set up on almost the same
plan. Durkheim was less than satisfied with it; he found it
difficult to reach an acceptable level of formulation in this
work. This is because the intellectual ideal of our democracy
is less well defined than its moral ideal; there has been less
scientific study of it, the subject is newer.

Here again there are two parts, of different orientations:
the one examines the end in view, the other, the means employed; the first asks sociology to define the intellectual type
that our society strives to realize; the other asks of logic and
of psychology what contribution each discipline makes, what
resources, what means, what resistances the mind of the
child offers to the educator working toward the realization
of this type. Among the purely psychological lectures, let
us note those that deal with attention; they are evidence of
what Durkheim was able to do when he applied himself to
psychology.

In order to assign a definite end to primary intellectual
education, Durkheim studies the origins of primary education and investigates how it has, in fact, become aware of
its proper nature and role. It developed later than secondary
education and was defined, to a degree, through opposition
to it. It is in two of its principal innovators, Comenius and
Pestalozzi, that Durkheim tries to grasp its ideal in process
of formation. Both asked how a system of education could
be simultaneously encyclopedic and elementary—to give an

46

idea of everything, to form an equitable and balanced mind, that is to say, able to grasp reality as a whole, without failing to appreciate any essential element of it—but also applying to all children without exception, of whom the majority will have to be content with summary notions, easy to assimilate rapidly. Through the critical interpretation of the efforts of Comenius and Pestalozzi, Durkheim elaborates his definition of the ideal to be realized. As is true of morality, the intellectual type required of the contemporary Frenchman demands the formation, in the individual, of a certain number of fundamental aptitudes. Durkheim calls them *categories*, master conceptions, foci of understanding, which are the frameworks and the tools of logical thought. He means by "categories" not only the most abstract forms of thought, the notion of cause or of substance, but ideas, richer in content, which govern our interpretation of reality: *our* idea of the physical world, *our* idea of life, *our* idea of man, for example. One does not see how these categories are innate in the human mind. They have a history; they have been built up, little by little, in the course of the evolution of civilization, and, in our civilization, by the development of the physical and moral sciences. A good mind is one whose dominant ideas, which govern the exercise of thought, are in harmony with the fundamental sciences as they are presently constituted; thus equipped, this mind can operate in the realm of the truth as we conceive it. The child must, then, be taught the elements of the fundamental sciences, or, rather, the fundamental disciplines, in order to show that grammar or history, for example, themselves co-operate, and in the highest degree, in the formation of the understanding.

Durkheim agrees, then, with so many great pedagogues in requiring what is called, barbarously, *formal* culture: to

47

form the mind, not fill it. It is not for its utility alone that learning is particularly worthwhile. There is nothing less utilitarian than this conception of education. But its formalism is original and is clearly opposed to that of a Montaigne, to that of the humanists. Indeed, the transmission through the teacher to the pupil of positive knowledge, the assimilation by the child of a *subject*, seem to him to be the condition of a real intellectual formation. And this is the reason: sociological analysis of understanding has pedagogical consequences. Memory, attention, the faculty of association, are congenital dispositions in the child, which exercise develops within the individual's own experience, whatever the object to which these faculties are applied. The guiding ideas elaborated by our civilization are, on the contrary, collective ideas that must be transmitted to the child, because he would not know how to elaborate them alone. One does not recreate science through one's own personal experience, because it is social and not individual; one learns it. No doubt it is not transmitted from one mind to another: it is the container itself, that is, intelligence, that is to be molded through and on science. Thus, although the guiding ideas are forms, it is not possible to transmit them empty. Auguste Comte had already said that one cannot study logic without science, the method of the sciences, without their theory, or be initiated into their spirit without assimilating some of their results. Durkheim thinks, with him, that it is necessary to learn about things, to acquire knowledge, disregarding the very value of learning, because learning is necessarily implied in the forms constitutive of the understanding.

To perceive all that Durkheim draws from these principles, it would be necessary to go into the details of the second part of the course. In it he studies, in turn, the teaching of some fundamental areas of instruction: mathematics and the categories of number and form; physics and the notion of reality; geography and the notion of the planetary milieu; history and the notions of historic duration and development. This enumeration is incomplete. Elsewhere, Durkheim has treated logical education through languages. He gives only examples. The collaboration of specialists, moreover, would be necessary to follow in detail all the consequences, for teaching, of the principles stated.

Take, for example, the notion of historic duration. History is the development, in time, of human societies. But this time infinitely surpasses the durations that the individual knows, of which he has direct experience. History cannot make sense to a mind which does not possess a certain conception of this historic duration; a good mind is above all one that possesses it. Now the child cannot, alone, construct this conception, the elements of which are not furnished to him by sensation or by individual memory. He must be helped, then, to construct it. In fact, this is one of the functions that historical instruction fulfills. But it does this, so to speak, without expressly intending to do so. It is remarkable that the teacher rarely senses the inanity of dates and the necessity to work systematically to give them meaning. The child is taught: Battle of Tolbiac, 496. How could the child attach a precise meaning to this date, when the conception of a past, even near, is so difficult for him? Considerable work is necessary, the stages of which might be the following: to give the idea of a century by adding, one to the other, the duration of three or four generations; that of the Christian era, by explaining why the birth of Christ was chosen as the beginning. Between the point of departure and the present epoch, give landmarks for duration by concrete reference points, biographies of personages or symbolic events. Set up, thus, a first sketch, the outline of which will be gradually filled in. Then show that the starting point of the era is arbitrary, that there are other

49

eras, other histories than ours, that these eras themselves exist in a duration to which human chronology does not apply, that the first beginnings escape us, etc. How few of us remember receiving, from our professors of history, lectures inspired by such principles. We have, indeed, finally acquired these notions; one cannot say that, save for exceptions, they had been methodically formed. One of the essential results of historical instruction, then, is attained, in fact, almost without being clearly perceived or desired. Now, the brevity of primary education requires that one come straight to the point, if this education is to be fully efficacious.

It may be said that, up to our time, grammatical and literary instruction is the only one that had become fully aware of its logical role: it teaches *in order to form;* the learning that it transmits is voluntarily used in the constitution of the understanding. In some measure, mathematical instruction is assigned the same role; here, however, the educational function which creates learning is often lost sight of, and the learning is appreciated in itself. One sees that Durkheim's conception of teaching is related to, while giving new form to, that of Herbart. Put in its place in the history of pedagogical theories, it seems to resolve the conflict between *formalism* and its opposite, the opposition between knowledge and culture. It provides the principle which alone will make it possible to resolve the difficulties with which our primary and secondary education is struggling, torn between encyclopedic aspirations and the fair sense of the dangers to which they give rise. Each of the fundamental disciplines implies a latent philosophy, that is to say, a system of cardinal notions which sum up the most general characteristics of things as we conceive them, and which govern their interpretation. It is this philosophy, product of the cumulative work of generations, that must be transmitted to the child, because it constitutes the very framework of the intelligence. *Philosophical* and *elementary* are not mutually exclusive terms. Quite to the contrary: the most elementary education must be the most philosophical. But it goes without saying that what is here called philosophy should not be expounded in abstract form. It should emerge from the most familiar teaching, without ever being formulated. But in order so to emerge, it must first inspire such teaching.

V

Elementary intellectual education is divided into two types, primary education for the mass, and secondary education for the elite. It is the education of the elite that raises, in contemporary France, the most embarrassing problems. For more than a century our secondary education has been going through a crisis, the result of which is still uncertain. One can speak without exaggeration of the social problem of secondary education. What is its exact nature and what is its role? What causes have determined the crisis, of what does it consist exactly, how can one foresee how it will be resolved? It is to the treatment of these questions that Durkheim devoted one of his finest courses, on "The Evolution and the Role of Secondary Education in France," a course that he taught several times, and of which he has left two completed versions. He had undertaken it at the request of Rector Liard, when the latter wanted to organize, for the first time, a course in pedagogy for the future secondary school teachers. Intended for candidates for all the *agrégations*,* both scientific and literary, its purpose was, in Durkheim's thinking, to arouse in everyone at the same time the

---

* After the *licence* (the first university degree) the French student may, after several years of study, take a highly competitive examination for the *agrégation*. The *agrégé*, one of a very small number of successful candidates each year, is assured of a teaching position in one of the better *lycées* (secondary schools).—Translator's note.

sentiment of the common task: an indispensable sentiment, if we want the various disciplines to co-operate in an instruction which, like the mind which it forms, must have its unity. It is probable that the future secondary school teachers will themselves feel, one day, the need to reflect systematically under the direction of a master, upon the proper nature and function of the institution which they must keep alive. And on that day, Durkheim's course will appear as the surest guide for this reflection. Its author deemed inadequate, at many points, the investigations that he had undertaken, the documentation on which he had relied. Let no one forget, before judging the work, that he devoted to this immense subject hardly more than one or two years of work. As it stands, this course is an incomparable model of what the application of sociological method to education can give. It is the only finished example that Durkheim was able to leave of the historical analysis of a system of scholastic institutions.

To understand the present secondary education of France, Durkheim observes how it was formed. The framework dates from the Middle Ages, when the Universities were founded. It is within the University, by the progressive introduction into the colleges of instruction given in the Faculty of Arts, that secondary education was born, becoming differentiated from higher education. Thus are explained their connections: the one prepared for the other. Dialectic instruction was, in the Middle Ages, the general propaedeutic because dialectics was then the universal method; formal instruction, general culture given by the aid of a very special discipline, it already had the characteristics which secondary education was to retain throughout the entire course of its history. But if the framework had been established since the Middle Ages, educational discipline changed in the sixteenth

century; for logic were substituted the Greco-Latin humani-
ties. Originating in the Renaissance, humanism, in France,
was given impetus particularly by the Jesuits. They put their
own mark on it; and although their rivals, the Oratory, Port-
Royal, University, had tempered their system, it is humanism as the Jesuits understood it that has been the educator
par excellence of the classic French spirit. In no European
society was the influence of humanism so exclusive: our
national spirit, through some of its dominant characteristics,
is expressed in it, and at the same time results from it, with
its virtues and its defects. But especially from the eighteenth
century, other tendencies were manifested: pedagogy, called
realist, violently attacked humanism. First it produced
theories, without direct effect on scholastic institutions. Then
it created, with the Central Schools of the Convention, a
completely new school system, the duration of which was
ephemeral. And the nineteenth century brought together
the old system and the new, without succeeding in eliminating one or the other, or in reconciling them definitively,
either. And it is still this conflict from which we are seeking
to escape. By helping us to understand it, history prepares
us to resolve it.

VI

Pedagogical instruction generally devotes much time to
the critical history of theories of education. Durkheim recognized the value of this study. He applied himself to it for a
long time. In the two courses on intellectual education,
primary and secondary, a place is given to the history of
theories; that of Comenius, among others, occupied his attention. He left outlines of lectures and notes for a course
which form a history of the principal pedagogical theories
in France since the Renaissance. *The Review of Meta-*

physics and Morality has published the plan developed for his lectures on Jean-Jacques Rousseau. Finally, he wrote out an entire course, for a whole year, on Pestalozzi and Herbart. Let us simply indicate here what method he followed.

First, he clearly distinguishes the history of theories of education from the history of education itself. These are often confused. But there are two things here, as distinct as the history of political philosophy and the history of political institutions. One might wish that our educators might better understand the history of our scholastic institutions and not think, as happens, that they come to know it through Rousseau or Montaigne.

Then, Durkheim particularly treats theories as facts, and it is the education of the historic spirit that he means to follow in studying them. It is quite otherwise, usually, that they are approached. Take, for example, the books of Gabriel Compayré, classic handbooks of the history of pedagogy, familiar to all our teachers. Despite their name, these are not, properly speaking, histories. No doubt they perform some service. But they recall, unfortunately, a certain conception of the history of philosophy, happily obsolete. It seems that the great pedagogues, a Rabelais, a Montaigne, a Rollin, a Rousseau, appear in them as collaborators of the theorist who now seeks to establish pedagogical theory. It would seem that there is an eternal pedagogical truth, universally valid, approximations to which they have presented. In their theory, one tries to separate the chaff from the wheat, to retain the precepts now useful for teachers, to reject their paradoxes and their errors. Dogmatic criticism takes precedence over history, praise or blame are more important than the interpretation of ideas. The residual intellectual gain is rather slim. It is not in the dialectic confrontation of theories of the past, theories which are rich in confused intuitions rather than scientifically constructed, that one has the opportunity to develop a solid and practically fruitful theory. It generally happens that second-rate theorists, eclectic, moderate, and reasonable in a rather dull way, withstand this criticism much better than first-rate minds. The wisdom of a Rollin is usefully opposed to the extravagances of a Rousseau. If pedagogy were a science, its history would have this strange characteristic, that genius would more often have led it into error, and mediocrity kept it in the path of truth.

Durkheim certainly understands that one can seek, through a critical discussion, to extract the elements of truth contained in a theory. In the Preface that he wrote for the posthumous book of Hamelin, *The System of Descartes,* he gave the formula for a method of interpretation, both historical and critical. And he applied this method himself to the study of Pestalozzi and Herbart. He liked the vigorous and rich thought of these great innovators, and, far from not recognizing its fruitfulness, he even asked himself if he did not attribute to them any of the ideas the first insights of which he believed he discerned in them. But, whatever their theoretical value may be, Durkheim especially asks that theories reveal the social forces that foster a system of education or work to modify it. The history of pedagogy is not the history of education, for the theorists do not express exactly what actually happens and do not foretell exactly what will actually take place. But ideas are also facts, and, when they are widely shared, social facts. The prodigious success of *Emile* has other causes than the genius of J.-J. Rousseau; it shows the confused but vigorous tendencies of the European society of the eighteenth century. There are conservative pedagogues, such as a Jouvency, a Rollin, who reflect the pedagogical ideals of the Jesuits or of the University of the seventeenth century. And above all, since one sees great theories abound in times of crisis, there are revolutionary pedagogues who interpret the collective phenomena which it is essential for the observer to get at, which it is almost impossible to get at directly: aspirations, ideals in process of formation, rebellions against institutions that have become decayed. For example, Durkheim studied, from this point of view, the pedagogical ideas of the Renaissance and distinguished, better than had ever been done before him, the two great currents that carry them—that which runs through the work of Rabelais, and the other, quite different, despite their overlapping, that runs through the work of Erasmus.

Such, in its broad outlines, is the pedagogical work of Durkheim. This brief exposition suffices to point up its scope and the close relations that it bears to his entire sociological work. To educators it brings, regarding the principal pedagogical problems, an original and vigorous theory. For sociologists it clarifies, on certain essential points, conceptions that Durkheim outlined elsewhere: relations between the individual and society, relations between science and practice, the nature of morality, and the nature of understanding. There are many educators and sociologists who ask that this pedagogical work not remain unpublished. The attempt will be made to publish the principal courses.

The little volume that we present today will serve as an introduction to them. We shall reprint in it the only pedagogical studies that Durkheim had published himself.* The

---

* We may mention, however: (1) the article "Childhood," in the *Dictionary of Pedagogy*, that Durkheim signed in collaboration with Buisson; (2) the communication on "Sexual Education," made to the French Philosophical Society (*Bulletin*), which is related above all to Durkheim's works on the family and marriage.

The posthumous study of *Emile*, which appeared in the *Review of Metaphysics and Morality*, Vol. XXVI, 1919, p. 153, cannot be separated from the study of *The Social Contract* (same *Review*, Vol. XXV, 1918).

first two reproduce the articles "Education" and "Pedagogy" in the *New Dictionary of Pedagogy and Primary Education,* published under the direction of F. Buisson, (Paris: Hachette, 1911); the third is the opening lecture given by Durkheim when he assumed his chair at the Sorbonne in 1902; it appeared in the *Review of Metaphysics and Morality* for January, 1903; the last is the opening lecture of the course organized for the candidates for the *agrégations* in secondary education; given in November, 1905, this lecture appeared in the *Political and Literary Review* (*Blue Review*) for January 20, 1906.

Some pages have repetitions; there are even, in the first two selections, textual borrowings from the third. We have thought that editing them would be more inconvenient than some repetitions.

Emile Durkheim

EDUCATION AND SOCIOLOGY

CHAPTER I

EDUCATION: ITS NATURE AND ITS ROLE

1. Definitions of education. Critical examination.

The word "education" has sometimes been used in a very broad sense to designate the totality of influences that nature or other men are able to exercise either on our intelligence or on our will. It includes, says John Stuart Mill, "all that we ourselves do and all that others do for us to the end of bringing us closer to the perfection of our nature. In its most widely accepted sense, it includes even indirect effects on the character and faculties of men produced by things having quite a different objective: by laws, by forms of government, the industrial arts, and even by physical phenomena, independent of human will, such as climate, soil, and locality." But this definition includes elements that are quite disparate, and that one cannot combine under a single heading without confusion. The influence of things on men is very different, in their processes and effects, from that which comes from men themselves; and the influence of peers on peers differs from that which adults exercise on youth. It is only the latter that concerns us here, and, therefore, it is this meaning that it is convenient to reserve for the word "education."

But what is the specific nature of this influence? Various answers have been given to this question; they can be divided into two main types.

Following Kant, "the end of education is to develop, in each individual, all the perfection of which he is capable." But what is meant by perfection? It is, as has often been said, the harmonious development of all the human faculties. To carry to the highest point that can be reached all the capacities that are in us, to realize them as completely as possible, without their interfering with one another, is not this an ideal beyond which there can be no other?

But if, to a degree, this harmonious development is indeed necessary and desirable, it is not wholly attainable; for it is in contradiction to another rule of human behavior which is no less cogent: that which has us concentrate on a specific, limited task. We cannot and we must not all be devoted to the same kind of life; we have, according to our aptitudes, different functions to fulfill, and we must adapt ourselves to what we must do. We are not all made for reflection; there is need for men of feeling and of action. Conversely, there is need of those whose job is thinking. Now, thought can develop only in detachment from action, only by turning in upon itself, only by turning its object entirely away from overt action. From this comes a first differentiation which is accompanied by a break of equilibrium. And behavior, in turn, as thought, can take a variety of different and specialized forms. Doubtless this specialization does not exclude a certain common base and, consequently, a certain balance of functions, organic and psychic alike, without which the health of the individual would be endangered, as well as social cohesion. We see, thus, that perfect harmony cannot be presented as the final end of conduct and of education.

Still less satisfactory is the utilitarian definition, according to which the objective of education would be to "make the individual an instrument of happiness for himself and for his fellows" (James Mill); for happiness is an essentially subjective thing that each person appreciates in his own way. Such a formula, then, leaves the end of education undetermined and, therefore, education itself, since it is left to individual fancy. Spencer, to be sure, tried to define happiness objectively. For him, the conditions of happiness are those of life. Complete happiness is the complete life. But what is meant by life? If it is a matter of physical existence alone, one may well say: that without which it would be impossible; it implies, in effect, a certain equilibrium between the organism and its environment, and, since the two terms in relation are definable data, it must be the same with their relation. But one can express, in this way, only the most immediate vital necessities. Now, for man, and above all for the man of today, such a life is not life. We ask more of life than normal enough functioning of our organs. A cultivated mind prefers not to live rather than give up the joys of the intellect. Even from the material point of view alone, everything over and above what is strictly necessary cannot be exactly determined. The "standard of life," as the English say, the minimum below which it does not seem to us that we can consent to descend, varies infinitely according to conditions, milieux, and the times. What we found sufficient yesterday, today seems to us to be beneath the dignity of man, as we define it now, and everything leads us to believe that our needs in this connection grow increasingly.

We come here to the general criticism that all these definitions face. They assume that there is an ideal, perfect education, which applies to all men indiscriminately; and it is this education, universal and unique, that the theorist tries to define. But first, if history is taken into consideration, one finds in it nothing to confirm such an hypothesis. Education has varied infinitely in time and place. In the cities of Greece and Rome, education trained the individual to subordinate himself blindly to the collectivity, to become the creature of society. Today, it tries to make of the individual an autonomous personality. In Athens, they sought to form cultivated souls, informed, subtle, full of measure and harmony, capable of enjoying beauty and the joys of pure speculation; in Rome, they wanted above all for children to become men of action, devoted to military glory, indifferent to letters and the arts. In the Middle Ages, education was above all Christian; in the Renaissance, it assumes a more lay and literary character; today science tends to assume the place in education formerly occupied by the arts. Can it be said, then, that the fact is not the ideal; that if education has varied, it is because men have mistaken what it should be? But if Roman education had been infused with an individualism comparable to ours, the Roman city would not have been able to maintain itself; Latin civilization would not have developed, nor, furthermore, our modern civilization, which is in part descended from it. The Christian societies of the Middle Ages would not have been able to survive if they had given to free inquiry the place that we give it today. There are, then, ineluctable necessities which it is impossible to disregard. Of what use is it to imagine a kind of education that would be fatal for the society that put it into practice?

This assumption, so doubtful, in itself rests on a more general mistake. If one begins by asking, thus, what an ideal education must be, abstracted from conditions of time and place, it is to admit implicitly that a system of education has no reality in itself. One does not see in education a collection of practices and institutions that have been organized slowly in the course of time, which are comparable with all the other social institutions and which express them, and which, therefore, can no more be changed at will than the structure of the society itself. But it seems that this would be a pure system of *a priori* concepts; under this heading it appears to be a logical construct. One imagines that men of each age organize it voluntarily to realize a determined end; that, if this organization is not everywhere the same, it is because mistakes have been made concerning either the end that it is to pursue or the means of attaining it. From this point of view, educational systems of the past appear as so many errors, total or partial. No attention need be paid to them, therefore; we do not have to associate ourselves with the faulty observation or logic of our predecessors; but we can and must pose the question without concerning ourselves with solutions that have been given, that is to say, leaving aside everything that has been, we have only to ask ourselves what should be. The lessons of history can, moreover, serve to prevent us from repeating the errors that have been committed.

In fact, however, each society, considered at a given stage of development, has a system of education which exercises an irresistible influence on individuals. It is idle to think that we can rear our children as we wish. There are customs to which we are bound to conform; if we flout them too severely, they take their vengeance on our children. The children, when they are adults, are unable to live with their peers, with whom they are not in accord. Whether they had been raised in accordance with ideas that were either obsolete or premature does not matter; in the one case as in the other, they are not of their time and, therefore, they are outside the conditions of normal life. There is, then, in each period, a prevailing type of education from which we cannot deviate without encountering that lively resistance which restrains the fancies of dissent.

Now, it is not we as individuals who have created the customs and ideas that determine this type. They are the product of a common life, and they express its needs. They are, moreover, in large part the work of preceding generations. The entire human past has contributed to the formation of this totality of maxims that guide education today; our entire history has left its traces in it, and even the history of the peoples who have come before. It is thus that the higher organisms carry in themselves the reflection of the whole biological evolution of which they are the end product. Historical investigation of the formation and development of systems of education reveals that they depend upon religion, political organization, the degree of development of science, the state of industry, etc. If they are considered apart from all these historic causes, they become incomprehensible. Thus, how can the individual pretend to reconstruct, through his own private reflection, what is not a work of individual thought? He is not confronted with a *tabula rasa* on which he can write what he wants, but with existing realities which he cannot create, or destroy, or transform, at will. He can act on them only to the extent that he has learned to understand them, to know their nature and the conditions on which they depend; and he can understand them only if he studies them, only if he starts by observing them, as the physicist observes inanimate matter and the biologist, living bodies.

Besides, how else to proceed? When one wants to determine by dialectics alone what education should be, it is necessary to begin by asking what objectives it must have.

But what is it that allows us to say that education has certain ends rather than others? We do not know *a priori* what is the function of respiration or of circulation in a living being. By what right would we be more well informed concerning the educational function? It will be said in reply that from all the evidence, its object is the training of children. But this is posing the problem in slightly different terms; it does not resolve it. It would be necessary to say of what this training consists, what its direction is, what human needs it satisfies. Now, one can answer these questions only by beginning with observation of what it has consisted of, what needs it has satisfied in the past. Thus, it appears that to establish the preliminary notion of education, to determine what is so called, historical observation is indispensable.

2. Definition of education.

To define education we must, then, consider, educational systems, present and past, put them together, and abstract the characteristics which are common to them. These characteristics will constitute the definition that we seek.

We have already determined, along the way, two elements. In order that there be education, there must be a generation of adults and one of youth, in interaction, and an influence exercised by the first on the second. It remains for us to define the nature of this influence.

There is, so to speak, no society in which the system of education does not present a twofold aspect: it is at the same time one and manifold.

It is manifold. Indeed, in one sense, it can be said that there are as many different kinds of education as there are different milieux in a given society. Is such a society formed of castes? Education varies from one caste to another; that of the patricians was not that of the plebeians; that of the Brahman was not that of the Sudra. Similarly, in the Middle Ages, what a difference between the culture that the young page received, instructed in all the arts of chivalry, and that of the villein, who learned in his parish school a smattering of arithmetic, song and grammar! Even today, do we not see education vary with social class, or even with locality? That of the city is not that of the country, that of the middle class is not that of the worker. Would one say that this organization is not morally justifiable, that one can see in it only a survival destined to disappear? This proposition is easy to defend. It is evident that the education of our children should not depend upon the chance of their having been born here or there, of some parents rather than others. But even though the moral conscience of our time would have received, on this point, the satisfaction that it expects, education would not, for all that, become more uniform. Even though the career of each child would, in large part, no longer be predetermined by a blind heredity, occupational specialization would not fail to result in a great pedagogical diversity. Each occupation, indeed, constitutes a milieu *sui generis* which requires particular aptitudes and specialized knowledge, in which certain ideas, certain practices, certain modes of viewing things, prevail; and as the child must be prepared for the function that he will be called upon to fulfill, education, beyond a certain age, can no longer remain the same for all those to whom it applies. That is why we see it, in all civilized countries, tending more and more to become diversified and specialized; and this specialization becomes more advanced daily. The heterogeneity which is thus created does not rest, as does that which we were just discussing, on unjust inequalities; but it is not less. To find an absolutely homogeneous and egalitarian education, it would be necessary to go back to prehistoric societies, in the structure of which there is no differentiation; and yet these kinds of societies represent hardly more than one logical stage in the history of humanity.

But, whatever may be the importance of these special educations, they are not all of education. It may even be said that they are not sufficient unto themselves; everywhere that one observes them, they vary from one another only beyond a certain point, up to which they are not differentiated. They all rest upon a common base. There is no people among whom there is not a certain number of ideas, sentiments and practices which education must inculcate in all children indiscriminately, to whatever social category they belong. Even in a society which is divided into closed castes, there is always a religion common to all, and, consequently, the principles of the religious culture, which is, then, fundamental, are the same throughout the population. If each caste, each family, has its special gods, there are general divinities that are recognized by everyone and which all children learn to worship. And as these divinities symbolize and personify certain sentiments, certain ways of conceiving the world and life, one cannot be initiated into their cult without acquiring, at the same time, all sorts of thought patterns which go beyond the sphere of the purely religious life. Similarly, in the Middle Ages, serfs, villeins, burgers and nobles received, equally, a common Christian education. If it is thus in societies where intellectual and moral diversity reach this degree of contrast, with how much more reason is it so among more advanced peoples where classes, while remaining distinct, are, however, separated by a less profound cleavage! Where these common elements of all education are not expressed in the form of religious symbols, they do not, however, cease to exist. In the course of our history, there has been established a whole set of ideas on human nature, on the respective importance of our different faculties, on right and duty, on society, on the individual, on progress, on science, on art, etc., which are the very basis of our national spirit; all education, that of the rich as well as that of the poor, that which leads to professional careers as well as that which prepares for industrial functions, has as its object to fix them in our minds.

From these facts it follows that each society sets up a certain ideal of man, of what he should be, as much from the intellectual point of view as the physical and moral; that this ideal is, to a degree, the same for all the citizens; that beyond a certain point it becomes differentiated according to the particular milieux that every society contains in its structure. It is this ideal, at the same time one and various, that is the focus of education. Its function, then, is to arouse in the child: (1) a certain number of physical and mental states that the society to which he belongs considers should not be lacking in any of its members; (2) certain physical and mental states that the particular social group (caste, class, family, profession) considers, equally, ought to be found among all those who make it up. Thus, it is society as a whole and each particular social milieu that determine the ideal that education realizes. Society can survive only if there exists among its members a sufficient degree of homogeneity; education perpetuates and reinforces this homogeneity by fixing in the child, from the beginning, the essential similarities that collective life demands. But on the other hand, without a certain diversity all co-operation would be impossible; education assures the persistence of this necessary diversity by being itself diversified and spe-

70

cialized. If the society has reached a degree of development such that the old divisions into castes and classes can no longer be maintained, it will prescribe an education more uniform at its base. If at the same time there is more division of labor, it will arouse among children, on the underlying basic set of common ideas and sentiments, a richer diversity of occupational aptitudes. If it lives in a state of war with the surrounding societies, it tries to shape people according to a strongly nationalistic model; if international competition takes a more peaceful form, the type that it tries to realize is more general and more humanistic. Education is, then, only the means by which society prepares, within the children, the essential conditions of its very existence. We shall see later how the individual himself has an interest in submitting to these requirements.

We come, then, to the following formula: *Education is the influence exercised by adult generations on those that are not yet ready for social life. Its object is to arouse and to develop in the child a certain number of physical, intellectual and moral states which are demanded of him by both the political society as a whole and the special milieu for which he is specifically destined.*

3. Consequences of the preceding definition: the social character of education.

It follows from the definition that precedes, that education consists of a methodical socialization of the young generation. In each of us, it may be said, there exist two beings which, while inseparable except by abstraction, remain distinct. One is made up of all the mental states that apply only to ourselves and to the events of our personal lives: this is what might be called the individual being. The other is a system of ideas, sentiments and practices which express in us, not our personality, but the group or different groups of which we are part; these are religious beliefs, moral beliefs and practices, national or professional traditions, collective opinions of every kind. Their totality forms the social being. To constitute this being in each of us is the end of education.

It is here, moreover, that are best shown the importance of its role and the fruitfulness of its influence. Indeed, not only is this social being not given, fully formed, in the primitive constitution of man; but it has not resulted from it through a spontaneous development. Spontaneously, man was not inclined to submit to a political authority, to respect a moral discipline, to dedicate himself, to be self-sacrificing. There was nothing in our congenital nature that predisposed us necessarily to become servants of divinities, symbolic emblems of society, to render them worship, to deprive ourselves in order to do them honor. It is society itself which, to the degree that it is firmly established, has drawn from within itself those great moral forces in the face of which man has felt his inferiority. Now, if one leaves aside the vague and indefinite tendencies which can be attributed to heredity, the child, on entering life, brings to it only his nature as an individual. Society finds itself, with each new generation, faced with a *tabula rasa*, very nearly, on which it must build anew. To the egoistic and asocial being that has just been born it must, as rapidly as possible, add another, capable of leading a moral and social life. Such is the work of education, and you can readily see its great importance. It is not limited to developing the individual organism in the direction indicated by its nature, to elicit the hidden potentialities that need only be manifested. It creates in man a new being.

This creative quality is, moreover, a special prerogative of human education. Anything else is what animals receive, if one can apply this name to the progressive training to which they are subjected by their parents. It can, indeed, foster the development of certain instincts that lie dormant in the animal, but such training does not initiate it into a new life. It facilitates the play of natural functions, but it creates nothing. Taught by its mother, the young animal learns more quickly how to fly or build its nest; but it learns almost nothing that it could not have been able to discover through its own individual experience. This is because animals either do not live under social conditions or form rather simple societies, which function through instinctive mechanisms that each individual carries within himself, fully formed, from birth. Education, then, can add nothing essential to nature, since the latter is adequate for everything, for the life of the group as well as that of the individual. By contrast, among men the aptitudes of every kind that social life presupposes are much too complex to be able to be contained, somehow, in our tissues, and to take the form of organic predispositions. It follows that they cannot be transmitted from one generation to another by way of heredity. It is through education that the transmission is effected.

However, it will be said, if one can indeed conceive that the distinctively moral qualities, because they impose privations on the individual, because they inhibit his natural impulses, can be developed in us only under an outside influence, are there not others which every man wishes to acquire and seeks spontaneously? Such are the divers qualities of the intelligence which allow him better to adapt his behavior to the nature of things. Such, too, are the physical qualities, and everything that contributes to the vigor and health of the organism. For the former, at least, it seems

73

that education, in developing them, may only assist the development of nature itself, may only lead the individual to a state of relative perfection toward which he tends by himself, although he may be able to achieve it more rapidly thanks to the co-operation of society.

But what demonstrates, despite appearances, that here as elsewhere education answers social necessities above all, is that there are societies in which these qualities have not been cultivated at all, and that in every case they have been understood very differently in different societies. The advantages of a solid intellectual culture have been far from recognized by all peoples. Science and the critical mind, that we rank so high today, were for a long time held in suspicion. Do we not know a great doctrine that proclaims happy the poor in spirit? We must guard against believing that this indifference to knowledge had been artificially imposed on men in violation of their nature. They do not have, by themselves, the instinctive appetite for science that has often and arbitrarily been attributed to them. They desire science only to the extent that experience has taught them that they cannot do without it. Now, in connection with the ordering of their individual lives they had no use for it. As Rousseau has already said, to satisfy the vital necessities, sensation, experience and instinct would suffice as they suffice for the animal. If man had not known other needs than these, very simple ones, which have their roots in his individual constitution, he would not have undertaken the pursuit of science, all the more because it has not been acquired without laborious and painful efforts. He has known the thirst for knowledge only when society has awakened it in him, and society has done this only when it has felt the need of it. This moment came when social life, in all its forms, had become too complex to be able to function otherwise than through the co-operation of reflective thought, that is to say, thought enlightened by science. Then scientific culture became indispensable, and that is why society requires it of its members and imposes it upon them as a duty. But in the beginning, as long as social organization is very simple and undifferentiated, always self-sufficient, blind tradition suffices, as does instinct in the animal. Therefore thought and free inquiry are useless and even dangerous, since they can only threaten tradition. That is why they are proscribed.

It is not otherwise with physical qualities. Where the state of the social milieu inclines public sentiment toward asceticism, physical education will be relegated to a secondary place. Something of this sort took place in the schools of the Middle Ages; and this asceticism was necessary, for the only manner of adapting to the harshness of those difficult times was to like it. Similarly, following the current of opinion, this same education will be understood very differently. In Sparta its object above all was to harden the limbs to fatigue; in Athens, it was a means of making bodies beautiful to the sight; in the time of chivalry it was required to form agile and supple warriors; today it no longer has any but a hygienic end, and is concerned, above all, with limiting the dangerous effects of a too intense intellectual culture. Thus, even the qualities which appear at first glance so spontaneously desirable, the individual seeks only when society invites him to, and he seeks them in the fashion that it prescribes for him.

We are now in a position to answer a question raised by all that precedes. Whereas we showed society fashioning individuals according to its needs, it could seem, from this fact, that the individuals were submitting to an insupportable tyranny. But in reality they are themselves interested in this submission; for the new being that collective influence, through education, thus builds up in each of us, represents what is best in us. Man is man, in fact, only because he lives in society. It is difficult, in the course of an article, to demonstrate rigorously a proposition so general and so important, and one which sums up the works of contemporary sociology. But first, one can say that it is less and less disputed. And more, it is not impossible to call to mind, summarily, the most essential facts that justify it.

First, if there is today an historically established fact, it is that morality stands in close relationship to the nature of societies, since, as we have shown along the way, it changes when societies change. This is because it results from life in common. It is society, indeed, that draws us out of ourselves, that obliges us to reckon with other interests than our own, it is society that has taught us to control our passions, our instincts, to prescribe law for them, to restrain ourselves, to deprive ourselves, to sacrifice ourselves, to subordinate our personal ends to higher ends. As for the whole system of representation which maintains in us the idea and the sentiment of rule, of discipline, internal as well as external—it is society that has established it in our consciences. It is thus that we have acquired this power to control ourselves, this control over our inclinations which is one of the distinctive traits of the human being and which is the more developed to the extent that we are more fully human.

We do not owe society less from the intellectual point of view. It is science that elaborates the cardinal notions that govern our thought: notions of cause, of laws, of space, of number, notions of bodies, of life, of conscience, of society, and so on. All these fundamental ideas are perpetually evolving, because they are the recapitulation, the resultant of all scientific work, far from being its point of departure as Pestalozzi believed. We do not conceive of

76

man, nature, cause, even space, as they were conceived in the Middle Ages; this is because our knowledge and our scientific methods are no longer the same. Now, science is a collective work, since it presupposes a vast co-operation of all scientists, not only of the same time, but of all the successive epochs of history. Before the sciences were established, religion filled the same office; for every mythology consists of a conception, already well elaborated, of man and of the universe. Science, moreover, was the heir of religion. Now, a religion is a social institution.

In learning a language, we learn a whole system of ideas, distinguished and classified, and we inherit from all the work from which have come these classifications that sum up centuries of experiences. There is more: without language, we would not have, so to speak, general ideas; for it is the word which, in fixing them, gives to concepts a consistency sufficient for them to be able to be handled conveniently by the mind. It is language, then, that has allowed us to raise ourselves above pure sensation; and it is not necessary to demonstrate that language is, in the first degree, a social thing.

One sees, through these few examples, to what man would be reduced if there were withdrawn from him all that he has derived from society: he would fall to the level of an animal. If he has been able to surpass the stage at which animals have stopped, it is primarily because he is not reduced to the fruit only of his personal efforts, but co-operates regularly with his fellow-creatures; and this makes the activity of each more productive. It is chiefly as a result of this that the products of the work of one generation are not lost for that which follows. Of what an animal has been able to learn in the course of his individual existence, almost nothing can survive him. By contrast, the results of human experience are preserved almost entirely and in detail, thanks to books, sculptures, tools, instruments of every kind that are transmitted from generation to generation, oral tradition, etc. The soil of nature is thus covered with a rich deposit that continues to grow constantly. Instead of dissipating each time that a generation dies out and is replaced by another, human wisdom accumulates without limit, and it is this unlimited accumulation that raises man above the beast and above himself. But, just as in the case of the cooperation which was discussed first, this accumulation is possible only in and through society. For in order that the legacy of each generation may be able to be preserved and added to others, it is necessary that there be a moral personality which lasts beyond the generations that pass, which binds them to one another: it is society. Thus the antagonism that has too often been admitted between society and individual corresponds to nothing in the facts. Indeed, far from these two terms being in opposition and being able to develop only each at the expense of the other, they imply each other. The individual, in willing society, wills himself. The influence that it exerts on him, notably through education, does not at all have as its object and its effect to repress him, to diminish him, to denature him, but, on the contrary, to make him grow and to make of him a truly human being. No doubt, he can grow thus only by making an effort. But this is precisely because this power to put forth voluntary effort is one of the most essential characteristics of man.

4. The role of the State in education.

This definition of education provides for a ready solution of the controversial question of the duties and the rights of the State with respect to education.

The rights of the family are opposed to them. The child, it is said, belongs first to his parents; it is, then, their responsibility to direct, as they understand it, his intellectual and moral development. Education is then conceived as an essentially private and domestic affair. When one takes this point of view, one tends naturally to reduce to a minimum the intervention of the State in the matter. The State should, it is said, be limited to serving as an auxiliary to, and as a substitute for, families. When they are unable to discharge their duties, it is natural that the State should take charge. It is natural, too, that it make their task as easy as possible, by placing at their disposal schools to which they can, if they wish, send their children. But it must be kept strictly within these limits, and forbidden any positive action designed to impress a given orientation on the mind of the youth.

But its role need hardly remain so negative. If, as we have tried to establish, education has a collective function above all, if its object is to adapt the child to the social milieu in which he is destined to live, it is impossible that society should be uninterested in such a procedure. How could society not have a part in it, since it is the reference point by which education must direct its action? It is, then, up to the State to remind the teacher constantly of the ideas, the sentiments that must be impressed upon the child to adjust him to the milieu in which he must live. If it were not always there to guarantee that pedagogical influence be exercised in a social way, the latter would necessarily be put to the service of private beliefs, and the whole nation would be divided and would break down into an incoherent multitude of little fragments in conflict with one another. One could not contradict more completely the fundamental end of all education. Choice is necessary: if one attaches

79

some value to the existence of society—and we have just seen what it means to us—education must assure, among the citizens, a sufficient community of ideas and of sentiments, without which any society is impossible; and in order that it may be able to produce this result, it is also necessary that education not be completely abandoned to the arbitrariness of private individuals.

Since education is an essentially social function, the State cannot be indifferent to it. On the contrary, everything that pertains to education must in some degree be submitted to its influence. This is not to say, therefore, that it must necessarily monopolize instruction. The question is too complex to be able to be treated thus in passing; we shall discuss it later. One can believe that scholastic progress is easier and quicker where a certain margin is left for individual initiative; for the individual makes innovations more readily than the State. But from the fact that the State, in the public interest, must allow other schools to be opened than those for which it has a more direct responsibility, it does not follow that it must remain aloof from what is going on in them. On the contrary, the education given in them must remain under its control. It is not even admissible that the function of the educator can be fulfilled by anyone who does not offer special guarantees of which the State alone can be the judge. No doubt, the limits within which its intervention should be kept may be rather difficult to determine once and for all, but the principle of intervention could not be disputed. There is no school which can claim the right to give, with full freedom, an antisocial education.

It is nevertheless necessary to recognize that the state of division in which we now find ourselves, in our country, makes this duty of the State particularly delicate and at the same time more important. It is not, indeed, up to the State to create this community of ideas and sentiments without which there is no society; it must be established by itself, and the State can only consecrate it, maintain it, make individuals more aware of it. Now, it is unfortunately indisputable that among us, this moral unity is not at all points what it should be. We are divided by divergent and even sometimes contradictory conceptions. There is in these divergences a fact which it is impossible to deny, and which must be reckoned with. It is not a question of recognizing the right of the majority to impose its ideas on the children of the minority. The school should not be the thing of one party, and the teacher is remiss in his duties when he uses the authority at his disposal to influence his pupils in accordance with his own preconceived opinions, however justified they may appear to him. But in spite of all the differences of opinion, there are at present, at the basis of our civilization, a certain number of principles which, implicitly or explicitly, are common to all, that few indeed, in any case, dare to deny overtly and openly: respect for reason, for science, for ideas and sentiments which are at the base of democratic morality. The role of the State is to outline these essential principles, to have them taught in its schools, to see to it that nowhere are children left ignorant of them, that everywhere they should be spoken of with the respect which is due them. There is in this connection an influence to exert which will perhaps be all the more efficacious when it will be less aggressive and less violent, and will know better how to be contained within wise limits.

5. The power of education. The means of influence.

After having determined the end of education, we must seek to determine how and to what extent it is possible to attain this end, that is to say, how and to what extent education can be efficacious.

This question has always been very controversial. For Fontenelle, "neither does good education make good character, nor does bad education destroy it." By contrast, for Locke, for Helvetius, education is all-powerful. According to the latter, "all men are born equal and with equal aptitudes; education alone makes for differences." The theory of Jacotot resembles the preceding.

The solution that one gives to the problem depends on the idea that one has of the importance and of the nature of the innate predispositions, on the one hand, and, on the other, of the means of influence at the disposal of the educator.

Education does not make a man out of nothing, as Locke and Helvetius believed; it is applied to predispositions that it finds already made. From another point of view, one can concede, in a general way, that these congenital tendencies are very strong, very difficult to destroy or to transform radically; for they depend upon organic conditions on which the educator has little influence. Consequently, to the degree that they have a definite object, that they incline the mind and the character toward narrowly determined ways of acting and thinking, the whole future of the individual finds itself fixed in advance, and there does not remain much for education to do.

But fortunately one of the characteristics of man is that the innate predispositions in him are very general and very vague. Indeed, the type of predisposition that is fixed, rigid, invariable, which hardly leaves room for the influence of external causes, is instinct. Now, one can ask if there is a single instinct, properly speaking, in man. One speaks, sometimes, of the instinct of preservation; but the word is inappropriate. For an instinct is a system of given actions, always the same, which, once they are set in motion by sensation, are automatically linked up with one another until they reach their natural limit, without reflection having to intervene anywhere; now, the movements that we make when our life is in danger do not at all have any such fixity or automatic invariability. They change with the situation; we adapt them to circumstances: this is because they do not operate without a certain conscious choice, however rapid. What is called the instinct of preservation is, after all, only a general impulse to flee death, without the means by which we seek to avoid it being predetermined once and for all. One can say as much concerning what is sometimes called, not less inexactly, the maternal instinct, the paternal instinct, and even the sexual instinct. These are drives in a given direction; but the means by which these drives are expressed vary from one individual to another, from one occasion to another. A large area remains reserved, then, for trial and error, for personal accommodations, and, consequently, for the effect of causes which can make their influence felt only after birth. Now, education is one of these causes.

It has been claimed, to be sure, that the child sometimes inherits a very strong tendency toward a given act, such as suicide, theft, murder, fraud, etc. But these assertions are not at all in accord with the facts. Whatever may have been said about it, one is not born criminal; still less is one destined from birth for this or that type of crime; the paradox of the Italian criminologists no longer counts many defenders today. What is inherited is a certain lack of mental equilibrium, which makes the individual refractory to coherent and disciplined behavior. But such a temperament does not predestine a man to be a criminal any more than to be an explorer seeking adventures, a prophet, a political innovator, an inventor, etc. As much can be said of any occupational aptitudes. As Bain remarked, "the son of a great philologist does not inherit a single word; the son of a great traveler can, at school, be surpassed in geography by the son of a miner." What the child receives from his parents are very general faculties: some force of attention, a certain amount of perseverance, a sound judgment, imagination, etc. But each of these faculties can serve all sorts of different ends. A child endowed with a rather lively imagination will be able, depending on circumstances, on the influences that will be brought to bear upon him, to become a painter or a poet, or an engineer with an inventive mind, or a daring financier. There is, then, a considerable difference between natural qualities and the special forms that they must take to be utilized in life. This means that the future is not strictly predetermined by our congenital constitution. The reason for this is easy to understand. The only forms of activity that can be transmitted by heredity are those which are always repeated in a sufficiently identical manner to be able to be fixed, in a rigid form, in the tissues of the organism. Now, human life depends on conditions that are manifold, complex, and, consequently, changing; it must itself, then, change and be modified continuously. Thus it is impossible for it to become crystallized in a definite and positive form. But only very general, very vague dispositions, expressing the characteristics common to all individual experiences, can survive and pass from one generation to another.

To say that innate characteristics are for the most part very general, is to say that they are very malleable, very flexible, since they can assume very different forms. Between the vague potentialities which constitute man at the

84

moment of birth and the well-defined character that he must become in order to play a useful role in society, the distance is, then, considerable. It is this distance that education has to make the child travel. One sees that a vast field is open to its influence.

But, to exert this influence, does it have adequate means?

In order to give an idea of what constitutes the educational influence, and to show its power, a contemporary psychologist, Guyau, has compared it to hypnotic suggestion; and the comparison is not without foundation.

Hypnotic suggestion presupposes, indeed, the following two conditions: (1) The state in which the hypnotized subject is found is characterized by its exceptional passivity. The mind is almost reduced to the state of a *tabula rasa*; a sort of void has been achieved in his consciousness; the will is as though paralyzed. Thus, the idea suggested, meeting no contrary idea at all, can be established with a minimum of resistance; (2) however, as the void is never complete, it is necessary, further, that the idea take from the suggestion itself some power of specific action. For that, it is necessary that the hypnotizer speak in a commanding tone, with authority. He must say: *I wish;* he must indicate that refusal to obey is not even conceivable, that the act must be accomplished, that the thing must be seen as he shows it, that it cannot be otherwise. If he weakens, one sees the subject hesitate, resist, sometimes even refuse to obey. If he so much as enters into discussion, that is the end of his power. The more suggestion goes against the natural temperament of the subject, the more will the imperative tone be indispensable.

Now, these two conditions are present in the relationships that the educator has with the child subjected to his influence: (1) The child is naturally in a state of passivity quite comparable to that in which the hypnotic subject is found artificially placed. His mind yet contains only a small number of conceptions able to fight against those which are suggested to him; his will is still rudimentary. Therefore he is very suggestible. For the same reason he is very susceptible to the force of example, very much inclined to imitation. (2) The ascendancy that the teacher naturally has over his pupil, because of the superiority of his experience and of his culture, will naturally give to his influence the efficacious force that he needs.

This comparison shows how far from helpless the educator is; for the great power of hypnotic suggestion is known. If, then, educational influence has, even in a lesser degree, an analogous efficacy, much may be expected of it, provided that one knows how to use it. Far from being discouraged by our impotence, we might well, rather, be frightened by the scope of our power. If teachers and parents were more consistently aware that nothing can happen in the child's presence which does not leave some trace in him, that the form of his mind and of his character depends on these thousands of little unconscious influences that take place at every moment and to which we pay no attention because of their apparent insignificance, how much more would they watch their language and their behavior! Surely, education cannot be very effective when it functions inconsistently. As Herbart says, it is not by reprimanding the child violently from time to time that one can influence him very much. But when education is patient and continuous, when it does not look for immediate and obvious successes, but proceeds slowly in a well-defined direction, without letting itself be diverted by external incidents and adventitious circumstances, it has at its disposal all the means necessary to affect minds profoundly.

At the same time, one sees what is the essential means of educational influence. What makes for the influence of the hypnotist is the authority which he holds under the circumstances. By analogy, then, one can say that education must be essentially a matter of authority. This important proposition can, moreover, be established directly. Indeed, we have seen that the object of education is to superimpose, on the individual and asocial being that we are at birth, an entirely new being. It must bring us to overcome our initial nature; it is on this condition that the child will become a man. Now, we can raise ourselves above ourselves only by a more or less difficult effort. Nothing is so false and deceptive as the Epicurean conception of education, the conception of a Montaigne, for example, according to which man can be formed while enjoying himself and without any other spur than the attraction of pleasure. If there is nothing somber in life and if it is criminal artificially to make it so in the eyes of the child, it is, however, serious and important; and education, which prepares for life, should share this seriousness. To learn to contain his natural egoism, to subordinate himself to higher ends, to submit his desires to the control of his will, to confine them within proper limits, the child must exercise strong self-control. Now, we restrain ourselves, we limit ourselves, only for one or the other of the following two reasons: because it is necessary through some physical necessity, or because we must do it on moral grounds. But the child cannot feel the necessity that imposes these efforts on us physically, for he is not faced directly with the hard realities of life which make this attitude indispensable. He is not yet engaged in the struggle; whatever Spencer may have said about it, we cannot leave him exposed to these too harsh realities. It is necessary, then, that he be already formed, in large part, when he really

87

encounters them. One cannot, then, depend on their influence to make him bow his will and acquire the necessary mastery over himself.

Duty remains. The sense of duty is, indeed, for the child and even for the adult, the stimulus *par excellence* of effort. Self-respect itself presupposes it. For, to be properly affected by reward and punishment, one must already have a sense of his dignity and, consequently, of his duty. But the child can know his duty only through his teachers or his parents; he can know what it is only through the manner in which they reveal it to him through their language and through their conduct. They must be, then, for him, duty incarnate and personified. Thus moral authority is the dominant quality of the educator. For it is through the authority that is in him that duty is duty. What is his own special quality is the imperative tone with which he addresses consciences, the respect that he inspires in wills and which makes them yield to his judgment. Thus it is indispensable that such an impression emanate from the person of the teacher.

It is not necessary to show that authority, thus understood, is neither violent nor repressive; it consists entirely of a certain moral ascendancy. It presupposes the presence in the teacher of two principal conditions. First, he must have will. For authority implies confidence, and the child cannot have confidence in anyone whom he sees hesitating, shifting, going back on his decisions. But this first condition is not the most essential. What is important above all is that the teacher really feels in himself the authority the feeling for which he is to transmit. It constitutes a force which he can manifest only if he possesses it effectively. Now, where does he get it from? Would it be from the power which he does have, from his right to reward and punish? But fear of chastisement is quite different from respect for authority. It has moral value only if chastisement is recognized as just even by him who suffers it, which implies that the authority which punishes is already recognized as legitimate. And this is the question. It is not from the outside that the teacher can hold his authority, it is from himself; it can come to him only from an inner faith. He must believe, not in himself, no doubt, not in the superior qualities of his intelligence or of his soul, but in his task and in the importance of his task. What makes for the authority which is so readily attached to the word of the priest, is the high idea that he has of his calling; for he speaks in the name of a god in whom he believes, to whom he feels himself closer than the crowd of the uninitiated. The lay teacher can and should have something of this feeling. He too is the agent of a great moral person who surpasses him: it is society. Just as the priest is the interpreter of his god, the teacher is the interpreter of the great moral ideas of his time and of his country. Let him be attached to these ideas, let him feel all their grandeur, and the authority which is in them, and of which he is aware, cannot fail to be communicated to his person and to everything that emanates from him. Into an authority which flows from such an impersonal source there could enter no pride, no vanity, no pedantry. It is made up entirely of the respect which he has for his functions and, if one may say so, for his office. It is this respect which, through word and gesture, passes from him to the child.

Liberty and authority have sometimes been opposed, as if these two factors of education contradicted and limited each other. But this opposition is factitious. In reality these two terms imply, rather than exclude, each other. Liberty is the daughter of authority properly understood. For to be free is not to do what one pleases; it is to be master of one-self, it is to know how to act with reason and to do one's duty. Now, it is precisely to endow the child with this self-mastery that the authority of the teacher should be employed. The authority of the teacher is only one aspect of the authority of duty and of reason. The child should, then, be trained to recognize it in the speech of the educator and to submit to its ascendancy; it is on this condition that he will know later how to find it again in his own conscience and to defer to it.

CHAPTER II

THE NATURE AND METHOD OF PEDAGOGY

The two words "education" and "pedagogy" have often been confused; they must, however, be carefully distinguished.

Education is the influence exerted on children by parents and teachers. This influence is always present and it is general. There is no period in social life, there is not, so to speak, even a moment in the day when the young generations are not in contact with their elders and when, therefore, they are not receiving from them some educational influence. For this influence does not make itself felt only in the very brief moments when parents or teachers are consciously, and by explicit teaching, communicating the results of their experience to those who come after them. There is an unconscious education that never ceases. By our example, by the words that we utter, by the actions that we perform, we constantly mold our children.

It is quite otherwise with pedagogy. This consists not of actions, but of theories. These theories are ways of conceiving of education, not ways of practicing it. Sometimes they are distinguished from practices in use to the point of

91

being opposed to them. The pedagogy of Rabelais, that of Rousseau or of Pestalozzi, are in opposition to the education of their times. Education is, then, only the subject of pedagogy. The latter consists of a certain way of reflecting on the phenomena of education.

This is what makes pedagogy, at least in the past, intermittent, while education is continuous. There are peoples who have not had pedagogy, properly speaking; it appears, too, only at a relatively advanced period in history. It is found in Greece only after the time of Pericles, with Plato, Xenophon, and Aristotle. It hardly existed in Rome. In the Christian societies, it is only in the sixteenth century that it produces important works; and the progress that it makes then slows down in the following century, to resume its full vigor only during the eighteenth century. This is because man does not always reflect, but only when it is necessary to reflect, and because the conditions for reflection are not always and everywhere given.

This being established, we must find out what are the characteristics of pedagogical reflection and of its products. Must we see in it properly scientific theories, and should we say of pedagogy that it is a science, the science of education? Or is it appropriate to give it another name, and what? The nature of pedagogical method will be understood very differently according to the answer given to this question.

I. That the phenomena of education, considered from a certain point of view, can be the object of a discipline which presents all the characteristics of other scientific disciplines, is, first, readily demonstrated.

Indeed, in order that one may be able to call a set of studies science, it is necessary and sufficient that they present the following characteristics:

(1) They must deal with verified, selected, observed

92

facts. A science, indeed, is defined by its object; it assumes, consequently, that this object exists, that one can point it out, in some way, mark out the place that it occupies in the whole of reality.

(2) These facts must have within themselves a sufficient homogeneity to be able to be classed in the same category. If they were irreducible to one another, there would be, not one science, but as many different sciences as distinct types of facts to study. It happens often enough in the case of sciences in their formative stages, that they embrace rather confusedly a plurality of different objects; this is the case, for example, with geography, with anthropology, etc. But this is never more than a transitory phase in the development of the sciences.

(3) Finally, science studies these facts to know them, and only to know them, in an absolutely disinterested fashion. We purposely use this rather general and vague word, *know*, without otherwise specifying what scientific knowledge can be. It is of little consequence, indeed, that the scientist attempts to establish types rather than to discover laws, that he limits himself to describing or that he seeks to explain. Science begins at the point where knowledge, whatever it may be, is sought for itself. No doubt, the scientist knows well that his discoveries will very probably be usable. It may even happen that he purposely directs his researches to this or that point because he has a hunch that they will thus be more profitable, that they will allow the satisfaction of urgent needs. But so far as he devotes himself to scientific investigation, he is disinterested in practical consequences. He says what is; he establishes what things are, and he stops there. He does not concern himself with knowing if the truths that he discovers will be agreeable or disconcerting, if it is good that the relations that he estab-

lishes remain what they are, or if it would be better that they were otherwise. His role is to express reality, not to judge it.

This being established, there is no reason for education not to become the object of an inquiry which might satisfy all these conditions and which, consequently, presents all the characteristics of a science.

Indeed, education, as practiced in a given society and considered at a given moment of its evolution, is a totality of practices, of ways of doing things, of customs which constitute perfectly defined facts and which have the same reality as other social facts. They are not, as has been believed for a long time, more or less arbitrary and artificial contrivances which owe their existence only to the capricious influence of indeterminate wills. They constitute, on the contrary, real social institutions. There is no man who can make a society have, at a given moment, a system of education other than that which is implied in its structure, just as it is impossible for a living organism to have other organs and other functions than those which are implied in its constitution. If, to all the reasons which have been given in support of this conception, it is necessary to add new ones, it is sufficient to take into consideration the imperative force with which these practices are imposed upon us. It is idle to believe that we raise our children as we wish. We are forced to follow the rules which prevail in the social milieu in which we live. Opinion imposes them on us, and opinion is a moral force whose constraining power is not less than that of physical forces. The practices to which it lends its authority are by that very fact beyond, to a great extent, the influence of individuals. We can, indeed, act contrary to them, but then the moral forces against which we are thus rebelling react against us, and it is difficult, because of their

94

superiority, for us not to be vanquished. It is thus that we can indeed revolt against the material forces on which we depend; we can try to live otherwise than the nature of our physical milieu implies; but then death or illness are the penalty of our revolt. In the same way, we are immersed in an atmosphere of collective ideas and sentiments which we cannot voluntarily modify; and it is on ideas and sentiments of this kind that educational practices rest. They are, then, phenomena distinct from us inasmuch as they resist us, realities which have in themselves a definite, given nature which is imposed on us; consequently, we can legitimately observe it, seek to know it with the sole end of knowing it. On the other hand, all educational practices, whatever they may be, whatever differences there may be among them, have in common one essential characteristic: they all follow from the influence exercised by one generation on the following generation with an eye to adapting the latter to the social milieu in which it is called upon to live. All educational practices are various modes of this fundamental relation. Therefore they are facts of the same kind, they fall into the same logical category; they can, then, serve as the object of one and the same science, which would be the science of education.

It is not impossible to indicate now, in order to make these ideas specific, some of the principal problems that this science would have to treat.

Educational practices are not phenomena that are isolated from one another; rather, for a given society, they are bound up in the same system all the parts of which contribute toward the same end: it is the system of education suitable to this country and to this time. Each people has its own, as it has its own moral, religious, economic system, etc. But on the other hand, peoples of the same kind, that is to say, people who resemble one another with respect to essential characteristics of their constitution, should practice comparable systems of education. The similarities in their general organization should necessarily lead to others of equal importance in their educational organization. Consequently, through comparison, by abstracting the similarities and eliminating the differences from them, one can certainly establish the generic types of education which correspond to the different types of societies. For example, under tribal conditions the essential characteristic of education is that it is diffuse; it is given to all the members of the clan indiscriminately. There are no specialized teachers, no special overseers entrusted with the training of the youth; it is all the elders, the totality of the ascending generations that play this role. At most it happens that, for certain particularly fundamental forms of instruction, certain elders are more specifically appointed. In other societies, more advanced, this diffuseness comes to an end or at least weakens. Education is concentrated in the hands of special functionaries. In India, in Egypt, it is the priests who are charged with this function. Education is an attribute of the priestly power. Now, this first differential characteristic leads to others. When the religious life, instead of itself remaining completely diffuse as it is originally, creates for itself a special organ charged with directing it and with administering it, that is to say, when it takes the form of a priestly class or caste, what is properly speculative and intellectual in religion takes a development unknown until then. It is in these priestly milieux that appeared the first precursors, the first and rudimentary forms of science: astronomy, mathematics, cosmology. This is a fact that Comte had noted a long time ago, and that is easily explained. It is quite natural that an organization the effect of which is to concentrate into a restricted group whatever speculative life then exists, should stimulate and develop it. Thus education is not limited, as in the beginning, to inculcating practices in the child, to training him in certain ways of behaving. There is from then on material for a specific instruction. The priest teaches the elements of those sciences which are in process of being formed. Only this knowledge, this speculative learning, are not taught for themselves, but by virtue of the relations that they have with religious beliefs; they have a sacred character, they are filled with properly religious elements, because they were formed in the very heart of religion and are inseparable from it. In other countries, as in the Greek and Latin cities, education remains divided, the proportions varying with the cities, between the State and the family. There is no priestly caste. It is the State that is responsible for religion. As it does not have speculative needs, as it is above all oriented toward action and practice, it is outside of the State, therefore also outside of religion, that science is born when the need for it becomes felt. The philosophers, the scientists of Greece, are private individuals and laymen. Science itself there very quickly assumes an antireligious tendency. The result is, from the point of view that interests us, that education too, as soon as it appears, has a lay and private character. The "grammateus" of Athens is a simple citizen, without official ties and without religious character.

It is useless to multiply these examples, which have only an illustrative interest. They suffice to show how, in comparing societies of the same type, one could establish types of education just as one establishes types of family, State or religion. This classification would not, moreover, exhaust the scientific problems that can be posed on the subject of education; it could only provide the necessary elements for resolving another, more important problem. Once the types were established, we would have to explain them, that is to say, to seek out the conditions on which the characteristic traits of each of them depended, and how they have emerged from one another. One would thus obtain the laws which govern the evolution of systems of education. One would be able to perceive, then, both how education developed and what the causes are which have determined this development and which account for it. A quite theoretical question, surely, but one the solution of which, one foresees readily, would be fruitful in practical applications.

Here already is a vast field of studies open to scientific speculation. And yet, there are still other problems which would be able to be attacked in the same spirit. Everything that we have just said relates to the past; the result of such researches would be to make us understand how our pedagogical institutions were established. But they can be considered from another point of view. Once formed, they function, and one could investigate how they function, that is to say, what results they produce and what are the conditions that make these results vary. For that a good set of scholastic statistics would be needed. There is in each school a discipline, a system of rewards and punishments. How interesting it would be to know, not only on the basis of empirical impressions, but through systematic observations, how this system functions in the different schools of the same locality, in different regions, at different times of the year, at different times of the day, what are the most frequent scholastic offenses, how their proportion varies over the whole territory or according to countries, how it depends on the age of the child, his family status, etc.! All the questions that are posed concerning the offenses of the adult can be posed here no less usefully. There is a criminology of the child, as there is a criminology of the adult man. And discipline is not the only educational institution which could be studied by this method. There is no pedagogical method whose effects could not be measured in the same way, on the assumption, of course, that the instrument necessary for such a study, that is to say, good statistics, has been established.

II. Here, then, are two groups of problems the purely scientific character of which cannot be disputed. One group relates to the genesis, the other to the functioning, of systems of education. In all these researches it is a matter simply either of describing present or past phenomena, or of inquiring into their causes, or of determining their effects. They constitute a science; this is what is, or rather, this is what would be, the science of education.

But even from the outline that we have just sketched, it is evident that the theories that are called pedagogical are speculations of quite another sort. Indeed, they neither follow the same end nor employ the same methods. Their objective is not to describe or to explain what is or what has been, but to determine what should be. They are oriented neither to the present nor to the past, but to the future. They do not propose to express existing reality as given, but to lay down precepts for conduct. They do not tell us this is what exists and what is the reason why, but tell us this is what must be done. Too, the theorists of education usually discuss the traditional practices of the present and of the past only with an almost systematic disdain. They point out their imperfections above all. Almost all the great pedagogues— Rabelais, Montaigne, Rousseau, Pestalozzi—are revolutionary spirits, rebels against the practices of their contemporaries. They mention the old or existing systems only to condemn them, to declare that they are without foundation in nature. They make of them a more or less complete *tabula rasa* and undertake to construct in their place something entirely new.

In order to make things quite clear, we must distinguish carefully two different kinds of speculation. Pedagogy is something other than the science of education. What is it, then? To make a reasoned choice, it is not enough for us to know what it is not; we must show what it is.

Shall we say that it is an art? This conclusion would appear to be obvious; for ordinarily one does not see any intermediate step between these two extremes and one gives the name "art" to any product of reflection which is not science. But this is to stretch the meaning of the word "art" to the point of including in it very different things.

Indeed, one also calls "art" the practical experience acquired by the teacher in contact with children and in the exercise of his profession. Now, this experience is manifestly a very different thing from the theories of the pedagogue. A fact of current observation makes this difference very apparent. One can be a fine teacher and yet be quite unsuited for the speculations of pedagogy. The skillful teacher knows how to do what must be done, without always being able to give the reasons that justify the procedures that he employs. Conversely, the pedagogue may lack all practical ability; we would have entrusted a class neither to Rousseau nor to Montaigne. Even of Pestalozzi, who, moreover, was himself an educator, one can say that he was probably not much of a teacher, as his repeated failures prove. The same confusion is found in other fields. One calls "art" the skill of the statesman, expert in the handling of public affairs. But one also says that the writings of Plato, of Aristotle, of Rousseau, are treatises on the art of politics; and we can certainly not see in them truly scientific works, since their object is not to study the real, but to construct an ideal. However, there is a wide gap between the mental processes that a book like the *Social Contract* implies and those that the administration of the State presupposes; Rousseau would very likely have been as poor a minister as an educator. It is thus, too, that the best theorists on medical matters are not the best clinicians, by far.

There is an advantage, then, in not denoting by the same word two forms of activity that are so different. It is necessary, we think, to reserve the name of art for everything that is pure practice without theory. It is this that everyone understands when one speaks of the art of the soldier, the art of the lawyer, the art of the teacher. An art is a system of ways of doing which are oriented to special ends and which are the product either of a traditional experience communicated by education, or of the personal experience of the individual. One can acquire them only by coming into contact with the things on which the action is to be performed and by dealing with them oneself. No doubt, it is possible that art may be illuminated by reflection, but reflection is not an essential element of it, since it can exist without reflection. Also, there is not a single art in which everything is reflected upon.

But between art so defined and science properly speaking, there is a place for an intermediate mental attitude. Instead of acting on things or on beings in a determinate way, one reflects on the processes of action which are thus employed, not to understand and explain them, but to appreciate what they are worth, if they are what they should be, if it is not useful to modify them, and in what way, and even more, to replace them completely with new procedures. These reflections take the form of theories; they are combinations of ideas, not combinations of acts, and in this they become closer to science. But the ideas which are so combined have, as their object, not to express the nature of things as given, but to direct action. They are not actions, but are closely related to actions which it is their function to orient. If they are not actions they are at least programs of action, and in this respect they are like art. Such are theories of medicine, politics, strategy, etc. To express the mixed character of these kinds of speculations, we propose to call them practical theories. Pedagogy is a practical theory of this type. It does not study systems of education scientifically, but it reflects on them in order to provide the activity of the educator with ideas to guide it.

III. But pedagogy, thus understood, is exposed to an objection the importance of which cannot be dissimulated. No doubt, it may be said, a practical theory is possible and legitimate when it can rest upon an established and undisputed science, of which it is only the application. In this case, indeed, the theoretical notions from which the practical consequences are deduced have a scientific value which is imparted to the conclusions that one draws from them. It is thus that applied chemistry is a practical theory which is only the putting into practice of the theories of pure chemistry. But a practical theory is worth only as much as the sciences from which it borrows its fundamental notions. Now, on what sciences can pedagogy rest? First there should be the science of education. For in order to know what education should be, it would be necessary, before anything, to know what its nature is, what are the diverse conditions on which it depends, the laws according to which it has evolved historically. But the science of education hardly exists except in embryonic form. There remain, on the one hand, the other branches of sociology which could aid pedagogy to fix the end of education, with the general orientation of method; on the other hand, psychology, the teachings of which could be very useful for the determination in detail of pedagogical procedures. But sociology is only a new science; it has only a very few established propositions, assuming that there are any at all. Psychology itself, although it was established earlier than the social sciences, is the object of all sorts of controversies; there are no psychological questions on which the most contradictory propositions are not still asserted. Consequently, what can practical conclusions be worth which rest on scientific data that are at the same time so uncertain and so incomplete? What can be the value of a pedagogical speculation which has no bases, or the bases of which, when they are not totally lacking, are so weak?

The fact that is thus invoked to discredit pedagogy is in itself indisputable. To be sure, the science of education has yet to be fully established, sociology and psychology are still not very well developed. If, then, we could wait, it would be prudent and methodical to be patient until these sciences would have made progress and would be able to be used with more assurance. But the problem is precisely that we may not be patient. We are not free to pose the problem to ourselves or to put it off; it is put to us, or rather imposed by phenomena themselves, by facts, by the necessity to live. This is not the whole story. We have begun, and we must go on. At many points our traditional system of education is no longer in harmony with our ideas and our needs. We have a choice, then, only between the following two alternatives: either try to preserve the practices that the past has left to us, anyway, even though they no longer answer the exigencies of the situation, or to undertake resolutely to re-establish the disturbed harmony by finding out what the necessary modifications are. Of these two alternatives, the first is not realizable and can come to nothing. Nothing is so fruitless as these attempts to give an artificial life and apparent authority to obsolete and discredited institutions. Failure is inevitable. One cannot stifle the ideas which these institutions contradict; one cannot silence the needs with which they clash. The forces against which one thus undertakes to fight cannot fail to win out.

We can only, then, set to work courageously, inquire into the changes which are indicated, and realize them. But how to discover them if not through reflection? Only the thinking mind can fill in the gaps in the tradition, when the latter has been faulty. Now, what is pedagogy if not reflection applied as systematically as possible to the phenomena of education, with the aim of regulating its development? No doubt, we do not have at our disposal all the elements that would be desirable for resolving the problem; but that is no reason for not seeking to resolve it—because it must be resolved. We can only do our best, collect as many instructive facts as we can, interpret them as methodically as we can, in order to reduce to a minimum the chances of error. Such is the role of the pedagogue. Nothing is so vain and sterile as that scientific puritanism which, under the pretext that science is not fully established, counsels abstention and recommends to men that they stand by as indifferent witnesses, or at least resigned ones, at the march of events. Beside the sophism of ignorance, there is the sophism of science which is not less dangerous. No doubt, to act under these conditions, one runs risks. But action never proceeds without risks; science, as advanced as it may be, would not know how to eliminate them. All that can be asked of us is to put all our science, as imperfect as it may be, and all our mental ability into the anticipation of these risks, as well as we can. And this is precisely what the role of pedagogy is.

But pedagogy will not be useful only in these critical

periods when it is urgently necessary to put a scholastic system back in harmony with the needs of the time; today, at least, it has become an indispensable auxiliary of education.

That is why, indeed, if the art of the educator is made up, above all, of instincts and almost instinctive practices, it nonetheless cannot do without intelligence. Reflection could not take its place, but it could not do without reflection, at least from the time when peoples have reached a certain degree of civilization. Indeed, once the individual personality has become an essential element of the intellectual and moral culture of humanity, the educator should take into account the germ of individuality that is in each child. He should seek to foster its development by all possible means. Instead of applying to all, in an invariable manner, the same impersonal and uniform set of rules, he should, on the contrary, vary and diversify his methods according to temperaments and the configuration of each intelligence. But to be able properly to adapt educational practices to the variety of individual cases, it is necessary to know what they are, what are the reasons for the different processes that constitute them, the effects which they produce in different circumstances; in a word, it is necessary to have them submitted to pedagogical reflection. An empirical, mechanical education cannot be other than repressive and leveling. On the other hand, to the degree that one advances in history, social evolution becomes more rapid; one period does not resemble the preceding one; each age has its own pattern. New needs and new ideas arise constantly; to be able to respond to the incessant changes which come about thus in opinions and customs, education itself must change and, consequently, must remain sufficiently flexible to allow for change. Now, the only way to prevent education from falling under the yoke of habit and from degenerating into mechanical and immutable automatism is to keep it constantly adaptable by reflection. When the educator takes account of the methods that he employs, of their end and their reason for being, he is in a position to judge them and thus he keeps himself ready to modify them if he becomes convinced that the end to pursue is no longer the same or that the means to employ should be different. Reflection is the force *par excellence* antagonistic to routine, and routine is the obstacle to necessary progress.

That is why, if it is true, as we said at the beginning, that pedagogy appears in history only intermittently, it is, however, necessary to add that it tends more and more to become a continuing function of social life. The Middle Ages had no need of it. It was a period of conformity in which everyone thought and felt in the same way, in which all minds were cast in the same mold, in which individual differences of opinion were rare and moreover, proscribed. Thus education was impersonal; the master in the medieval schools addressed himself to all the pupils collectively, without having the notion of adapting his teaching to the nature of each. At the same time, the immutability of the fundamental beliefs was opposed to any rapid evolution of the educational system. For these two reasons he had less need to be guided by pedagogical thought. But in the Renaissance everything changes: individual personalities emerge from the social mass in which they had, until then, been thoroughly immersed; minds become diversified; at the same time historical development accelerates; a new civilization is formed. To meet all these changes pedagogical reflection arises and, although it has not always been maintained at the same level, it was no longer to become completely extinguished.

IV. But in order that pedagogical reflection may be able

to produce the useful effects that one has a right to expect of it, it must be properly cultivated.

(1) We have seen that pedagogy is not education and could not take its place. Its role is not to substitute for practice, but to guide it, enlighten it, help it, if necessary, to fill the gaps which have been produced in it, to remedy its inadequacies. The pedagogue, then, does not have to construct a whole new system of education as if there were none before him; but he must, on the contrary, apply himself above all to knowing and understanding the system of his time; it is on this condition that he will be in a position to use it with discernment and to judge what is defective in it.

But to be able to understand it, it is not enough to consider it as it is today, for this system of education is a product of history that history alone can explain. It is indeed a social institution. Too, there is hardly any in which the entire history of the country is so completely reflected. The French schools interpret and express the French spirit. One can understand nothing of what they are, of the end that they pursue, if one does not know what constitutes our national spirit, what its various elements are, which are those that depend on permanent and profound causes, and which, by contrast, are due to the effect of more or less accidental and transitory factors—these are all questions which historical analysis alone can resolve. Much discussion centers around what place should be assigned to the primary school within the totality of our scholastic organization and within the general life of the society. But the problem is insoluble if one does not know how our scholastic organization was formed, whence come its distinctive characteristics, what has determined, in the past, the place which has been given in it to the elementary school, what are the causes that have fostered it or hindered its development, etc.

Thus, the history of education, at least of the national

107

education, is the first of the propaedeutics of a pedagogic culture. Naturally, if it is a matter of primary pedagogy, it is the history of primary education that one must know. But for the reason which we have just indicated, it could not be isolated from the wider scholastic system of which it is only one part.

(2) But this scholastic system is not made up solely of established practices, of methods consecrated by use, the heritage of the past. There are found in it, further, tendencies toward the future, aspirations toward a new ideal, more or less clearly foreseen. It is important to know these aspirations well in order to be able to appreciate what place they should have in scholastic reality. Now, they find expression in pedagogical doctrines; the history of these doctrines should, then, complete that of education.

One could believe, to be sure, that to fulfill its useful end this history does not need to go back very far into the past and can, without inconvenience, be very brief. Is it not enough to know the various conflicting theories of the present time? All the others, those of previous centuries, are today out of date and, it seems, no longer have any but an academic interest.

But we believe this modernism can only rarefy one of the principal sources by which pedagogical reflection should be maintained.

Indeed, the most recent theories were not born yesterday; they are the product of those which preceded, without which, consequently, they cannot be understood; and so, step by step, in order to discover the causes determining a pedagogical current of any importance, it is generally necessary to go back far enough into the past. It is on this condition, too, that one will have some assurance that the new views which arouse the keenest interest are not brilliant improvisations, destined to sink rapidly into oblivion. For example, to be able to understand the present trend toward teaching through demonstrations, toward what one may call pedagogical realism, one must not be content with seeing how it is expressed by this or that contemporary; one must go back to the time when it begins, that is to say, to the middle of the eighteenth century in France and toward the end of the seventeenth century in certain Protestant countries. Only in this way, by finding itself thus related to its first origins, will realist pedagogy be presented in quite a different light; one will better understand that it stems from profound, impersonal causes operating among all the peoples of Europe. And at the same time one will be in a better position to perceive what these causes are and, therefore, to judge the true scope of this movement. But on the other hand, this pedagogical current was established in opposition to a contrary current, that of humanistic and bookish education. Therefore one will be able judiciously to appreciate the first only on condition of also knowing the second; and so we are obliged to go still further back into history. This history of pedagogy, to be most fruitful, should not, furthermore, be separated from the history of education. Although we have distinguished them in the exposition, they are really interrelated. For at each moment of time, the theories depend on the state of education, which they reflect even though they react against it; and moreover, to the extent that they exercise an efficacious influence they contribute to determining it.

The pedagogic culture, then, should have a largely historical basis. It is on this condition that pedagogy will be able to avoid a criticism that has often been made of it and which has strongly prejudiced its influence. Too many pedagogues, including the most outstanding, have undertaken to erect their systems without considering what had existed before them. The treatment to which Ponocrates submits Gargantua before initiating him into new methods is significant on this point: he cleanses his brain "with Anticyrian hellebore" in such a way as to make him forget "everything that he had learned under his former teachers." That meant, in an allegorical form, that the new pedagogy was to have nothing in common with that which had preceded. But it meant by the same token that he was ignoring actual conditions. The future cannot be evoked from nothing; we can build it only with the materials that the past has bequeathed to us. An ideal that one constructs taking the reverse of the existing state of affairs is not realizable since it has no roots in reality. Besides, it is clear that the past had its reasons for being; it would not have been able to last if it had not answered legitimate needs which would not disappear completely overnight; one cannot ignore the past so completely without disregarding vital necessities. That is how it comes about that pedagogy has too often been only a form of utopian literature. We would pity children to whom the method of Rousseau or that of Pestalozzi would be rigorously applied. No doubt, these utopias have been able to play a useful role in history. Their very simplicism has allowed them to impress men more vividly and to stimulate them to action. But first, these advantages are not without drawbacks; further, for this everyday pedagogy which each teacher needs to illuminate and guide his daily practice, less emphatic and unilateral training is necessary and, on the contrary, more method, a keener awareness of reality and of the multiple difficulties which must be faced. It is this awareness that a well-understood historical culture will give.

(3) Only the history of education and of pedagogy allows for the determination of the ends that education

should pursue at any given time. But as for the means necessary to the realization of these ends, it is psychology that must be consulted.

Indeed, the pedagogical ideal for a period expresses above all the state of the society in the period under consideration. But in order that this ideal may become a reality, it remains necessary to mold the conscience of the child to it. Now, the conscience has its own laws which one must know to be able to modify them, at least if one wishes to try to avoid the empirical gropings which it is precisely the object of pedagogy to reduce to a minimum. To be able to stimulate activity to develop in a certain direction, one must also know what its causes are and what their nature is; for it is on this condition that it will be possible to exert the appropriate influence, based on knowledge. Is it a matter, for example, of arousing either patriotism or the sense of humanity? We shall know all the better how to shape the moral sensibility of the pupils in one or the other direction when we shall have more complete and more precise notions about the totality of phenomena that are called tendencies, habits, desires, emotions, etc., of the divers conditions on which they depend, and of the form that they take in the child. According to whether one sees in such tendencies a product of agreeable or disagreeable experiences that the species has been able to have, or on the contrary, a primitive fact prior to the affective states which accompany their functioning, one will have to treat them in very different ways in order to regulate their functioning. Now it is up to psychology, and more specifically, child psychology, to resolve these questions. If it is incompetent to fix the end—since the end varies with social conditions—there is no doubt that it has a useful role to play in the establishment of methods. And since no method can be applied in the same fashion to different children, it is psychology, too, that should help us to cope with the diversity of intelligence and character. We know, unfortunately, that we are still far from the time when it will truly be in a position to satisfy this desideratum.

There is a special form of psychology which has a very particular importance for the pedagogue: it is collective psychology. A class, indeed, is a small society, and it must not be conducted as if it were only a simple agglomeration of subjects independent of one another. Children in class think, feel and behave otherwise than when they are alone. There are produced, in a class, phenomena of contagion, collective demoralization, mutual over-excitement, wholesome effervescence, that one must know how to discern in order to prevent or to combat some and to utilize others. Although this science is still very young, it now includes a certain number of propositions which it is important not to ignore.

Such are the principal disciplines which can awaken and cultivate pedagogical reflection. Instead of seeking to lay down for pedagogy an abstract code of methodological rules —an undertaking which, in a mode of speculation so multiform and so complex, is hardly realizable in a satisfactory manner—it has seemed to us preferable to indicate how we think the pedagogue should be formed. A certain mental attitude toward the problems he is to treat is thus determined.

CHAPTER III

PEDAGOGY AND SOCIOLOGY

Gentlemen:

It is a very great honor for me, one the value of which I feel very strongly, to have to replace, in this chair, the man of high reason and of firm will to whom France owes so much for the improvement of her primary education. In close contact with the teachers of our schools for the fifteen years that I taught pedagogy at the University of Bordeaux, I was able to see at first hand the work with which the name of M. Buisson will remain definitively associated, and I know, therefore, its whole scope. Above all, when one thinks back to the state in which this system of education was found at the time when its reform was undertaken, it is impossible not to admire the importance of the results obtained and the rapidity of the progress accomplished. The schools multiplied and materially transformed, rational methods substituted for the old routines of bygone times, a new impetus given to pedagogical reflection, a general stimulation of initiative—all that certainly constitutes one of the greatest and most fortunate revolutions which have been produced in the history of our national education. It was very fortunate for science, then, when M. Buisson, judging

his task achieved, gave up his absorbing functions to communicate to the public, through teaching, the results of his
incomparable experience. Such great practical experience,
enlightened, moreover, by a broad philosophy, at once prudent and curious about all innovations, necessarily gave to
his word an authority which the moral prestige attached to
his person and the memory of the services rendered in all
the great causes to which M. Buisson devoted his life, came
to enhance.

I bring to you nothing like such a distinctive com-
petence. Thus, I should have cause to feel singularly frightened before the difficulties of my task, if I did not reassure
myself a bit with the thought that such complex problems
can be usefully studied by many minds and different points
of view. As a sociologist, it is above all as a sociologist that
I shall speak to you of education. Moreover, in proceeding
in this way, far from handling phenomena with a biased
frame of reference, I am, on the contrary, convinced that
there is no method better suited to demonstrating their true
nature. Indeed, I regard as the prime postulate of all pedagogical speculation that education is an eminently social
thing in its origins as in its functions, and that, therefore,
pedagogy depends on sociology more closely than on any
other science. And since this idea will dominate all my
teaching, as it already dominated the similar instruction that
I formerly gave at another university, it seemed to me
appropriate to use this first lecture to set it forth specifically
in order that you might be better able to follow its ultimate
applications. There can be no question of demonstrating it
explicitly in the course of only a single lecture. A principle
so general, the implications of which are so extensive, can
be verified only progressively, successively as one gets into
detailed facts and as one sees how it is applied to them. But

what is possible now is to give you an overview of the whole; to indicate to you the principal reasons for its acceptance from the first step of the inquiry, even if only provisionally and subject to the necessary verification; finally, to mark out its scope as well as its limits—and this will be the object of this first lecture.

I

It is all the more necessary immediately to call your attention to this fundamental axiom because it is not very generally known. Until recently—and there are still exceptions—modern pedagogues agreed almost unanimously that education is an eminently individual thing, and, consequently, on making of pedagogy an immediate and direct corollary of psychology alone. For Kant as for Mill, for Herbart as for Spencer, the object of education would be above all to realize, in each individual, but carrying them to their highest possible point of perfection, the attributes distinctive of the human species in general. They stated as a truism that there is one education and one alone, which, to the exclusion of any other, is suitable for all men indiscriminately, whatever may be the historical and social conditions on which they depend—and it is this abstract and unique ideal that the theorists of education propose to determine. They assumed that there is *one* human nature, the forms and properties of which are determinable once and for all, and the pedagogical problem consisted of investigating how the educational influence should be exercised on human nature so defined. No doubt, no one has ever thought that man is, at the outset, as soon as he enters life, all that he can and should be. It is quite clear that the human being is formed only progressively in the course of a slow growth which begins at birth and is completed only at

115

maturity. But they supposed that this growth is only a realization of potentialities and only brings to light the latent energies which existed, fully formed, in the physical and mental organism of the child. The educator, then, would have nothing essential to add to the work of nature. He would create nothing new. His role would be limited to preventing these existing potentialities from becoming atrophied through disuse, or from deviating from their normal direction, or from developing too slowly. Therefore, conditions of time and place, the state of the social milieu, lose all interest for pedagogy. Since man carries in himself all the potentialities of his development, it is he and he alone who must be observed when one undertakes to determine in what direction and in what manner this development should be guided. What is important is to know what his native faculties are and what their nature is. Now, the science which has as its object the description and explanation of the individual man is psychology. It seems, then, that it should suffice for all the needs of the pedagogue.

Unfortunately, this conception of education stands in absolute contradiction to all that history teaches us: there is not a people, indeed, among whom it has ever been put into practice. First of all, far from there being one education universally valid for the whole human species, there is, so to speak, no society in which different pedagogical systems do not coexist and function side by side. Is the society formed of castes? Education varies from one caste to another: that of the patricians was not that of the plebeians, that of the Brahman was not that of the Sudra. Similarly, in the Middle Ages, what a difference between the culture that the young page received, instructed in all the arts of chivalry, and that of the villein who learned in his parish school a smattering of arithmetic, song and grammar! Even today, do we not see education vary with social class or even with locality? That of the city is not that of the country, that of the middle class is not that of the worker. Would one say that this organization is not morally justifiable, that one can see in it only a survival destined to disappear? This proposition is easy to defend. It is evident that the education of our children should not depend upon the chance of their having been born here rather than there, of certain parents and not of others. But even though the moral conscience of our time would have received on this point the satisfaction that it expects, education would not, for all that, become more uniform. Even though the career of each child would no longer be predetermined, at least in large part, by a blind heredity, occupational specialization would not fail to result in a great pedagogical diversity. Each occupation, indeed, constitutes a milieu *sui generis* which requires particular aptitudes and specialized knowledge, in which certain ideas, certain practices, certain modes of viewing things, prevail; and as the child must be prepared for the function that he will be called upon to fulfill, education, beyond a certain age, can no longer remain the same for all those to whom it applies. That is why we see it in all civilized countries tending more and more to become diversified and specialized; and this specialization becomes more advanced daily. The heterogeneity which is thus created does not rest, as does that which we were just discussing, on unjust inequalities; but it is not less. To find an absolutely homogeneous and egalitarian education, it would be necessary to go back to prehistoric societies which are undifferentiated in structure, and yet these kinds of societies represent hardly more than one logical stage in the history of humanity.

Now, it is evident that these special educations are by no means organized in terms of individual ends. No doubt, it sometimes happens that they have the effect of developing in the individual particular aptitudes which were innate in him and which needed only to become active; in this sense, one can say that they help him to realize his nature. But we know how exceptional these callings, narrowly defined, are. In most cases, we are not predestined by our intellectual or moral temperament for a given function. The average man is eminently plastic; he can be equally well used in widely varied occupations. If, then, he specializes, and if he specializes in a given form rather than in some other, it is not for reasons which are within him; he is not forced to it by the necessities of his nature. But it is society which, to be able to maintain itself, requires that labor be divided among its members and be divided among them in a given fashion rather than another. This is why it creates for itself, by means of education, the specialized workers whom it needs. It is, then, for and through society that education is thus diversified.

There is more. Far from this special culture necessarily bringing us closer to human perfection, it does not work perfectly even though it is in harmony with the natural predispositions of the individual. For we cannot develop with the necessary intensity the faculties that our function specially implies, without letting the others atrophy in inaction, without giving up, therefore, a whole part of our nature. For example, man, as an individual, is made no less for acting than for thinking. Too, since he is above all a living being and since life is action, the active faculties are perhaps more essential to him than the others. And yet, from the moment when the intellectual life of societies has reached a certain degree of development, there are, and there must necessarily be, men who devote themselves exclusively to it, who do nothing but think. Now, thought can develop only in detachment from action, only by turning in on itself, by

turning its object away from action. Thus are formed those
incomplete natures in which all the energies of activity have
been, so to speak, converted into reflection, and which,
moreover, however incomplete they may be in certain respects, constitute the indispensable agents of scientific
progress. The abstract analysis of the human constitution
would never have made possible the prediction that man
was susceptible to change in this manner what passes for
being his essence, nor that an education was necessary to
bring about these useful alterations.

However, whatever may be the importance of these special educations, it is indisputable that they are not all of
education. It may even be said that they are not sufficient
unto themselves; everywhere that they are found, they vary
from one another only beyond a certain point, up to which
they are not differentiated. They all rest upon a common
base. There is no people, indeed, among whom there do not
exist a certain number of ideas, sentiments and practices
which education must inculcate in all children indiscriminately, to whatever social category they belong. It is
precisely this common education which generally passes for
the true education. It alone seems fully to deserve to be
called by this name. One grants to it, over all the others, a
kind of pre-eminence. It is, then, especially important to
know if, as is claimed, this common education is implied
as a whole in the notion of man and if it can be deduced
from this notion.

Actually, this question is not even posed with respect
to the systems of education which history tells us about.
They are so obviously tied up with given social systems that
they are inseparable from them. If, in spite of the differences
that separated the patriciate from the plebs, there was at
Rome an education common to all Romans, this education
had to be essentially Roman in character. It implied the

whole organization of the city at the same time that it was
its base. And what we say of Rome could be repeated of all
historical societies. Each type of people has its own education which is appropriate to it and which can serve to define
it in the same way as its moral, political and religious organization. Its education is one of the elements of its structure. That is why education has varied so prodigiously in
time and space; why here it habituates the individual completely to subordinate his personality to the State, while
elsewhere, on the contrary, it endeavors to make him an
autonomous being, controlling his own behavior; why it was
ascetic in the Middle Ages, liberal in the Renaissance,
literary in the seventeenth century, scientific in our time. It
is not because, by a series of aberrations, men have been
mistaken as to their nature as men and as to their needs, but
because their needs have varied—and they have varied because the social conditions on which human needs depend
have not remained the same.

But through an unconscious contradiction, what one
grants readily for the past one refuses to admit for the
present, and, still more, for the future. Everyone readily
sees that in Rome, in Greece, the unique object of education was to make Greeks and Romans and, consequently,
education was harmonious with the whole pattern of political, moral, economic and religious institutions. But we are
pleased to believe that our modern education is an exception to the common law, that from now on it is less directly
dependent upon social contingencies and that it is called
upon to free itself from them completely in the future. Do
we not repeat endlessly that we want to make men of our
children even before making citizens of them, and does it
not seem that our human quality is naturally independent
of collective influences since it is logically prior to them?

And moreover, would it not be a sort of miracle if education, after having had for centuries and in all known societies all the characteristics of a social institution, had been able so completely to change its nature? Such a transformation will seem still more surprising if one considers that the moment when it would have been accomplished is precisely that in which education has begun to become a true public service; for it is since the end of the last century that we see it, not only in France, but in all Europe, tending to come more and more directly under the control and the direction of the State. No doubt, the ends that it pursues are every day more detached from the local or ethnic conditions which distinguished them formerly; they become more general and more abstract. But they do not remain less essentially collective. Is it not, indeed, the collectivity that imposes them upon us? Is it not the collectivity that bids us develop above all in our children the qualities which are common to them with all men? There is more. Not only does it exert on us, through opinion, a moral pressure so that we may thus understand our duties as educators, but it attaches to it such a value that, as I have just indicated, the collectivity itself assumes the task. It is easily seen that if the collectivity cares this much about it, the reason is that it feels itself interested in the task. And, indeed, only a broadly human culture can give to modern societies the citizens whom it needs. Because each of the great European peoples covers a vast area, because it is recruited from the most diverse stocks, because there is an extreme division of labor in it, the individuals who compose it are so different from one another that there remains hardly anything in common among them, except their human quality in general. They can preserve the homogeneity indispensable to any social *consensus* only on the condition of being as equal as possible in the single respect in which they all resemble one another, that is to say, so far as they are all human beings. In other

121

words, in societies so differentiated, there can hardly be any collective type other than the generic type of man. Let it come to lose something of its generality, let it revert to the old particularism, and one will see these great States resolve into a multitude of little atomized groups and decompose. Thus our pedagogic ideal is explained by our social structure, just as that of the Greeks and of the Romans could be understood only through the organization of the city. If our modern education is no longer narrowly national, it is in the constitution of modern nations that the reason must be sought.

This is not all. Not only is it society which has raised the human type to the dignity of a model that the educator must attempt to reproduce, but it is society, too, that builds this model, and it builds it according to its needs. For it is an error to think that it may be given as a whole in the natural constitution of man, that it was only a matter of discovering it in him through methodical observation, except to embellish it afterwards by imagination in carrying to their highest development, through thought, all the potentialities which are found in it. The man whom education should realize in us is not the man such as nature has made him, but as the society wishes him to be; and it wishes him such as its internal economy calls for. What proves this is the manner in which our conception of man has varied from one society to another. For the ancients also believed in making men of their children, just as we do. If they refused to see their fellow-creature in the stranger, it is precisely because in their eyes the education of the city alone could make beings truly and properly human. Only they conceived humanity in their fashion, which is no longer ours. Every change of any importance in the organization of a society results in a change of the same importance in the idea that man makes of himself. When, under pressure of increased competition, the division of labor increases, when the specialization of each worker is at the same time more marked and more advanced, the universe of discourse of common education will necessarily be limited and, therefore, the characteristics of the human type will also become limited. Formerly, literary culture had been considered as an essential element of all human culture; and now we are approaching a time when it will itself no longer, perhaps, be more than a specialty. In the same way, if there exists a recognized hierarchy among our faculties, if there are some to which we attribute a sort of pre-eminence and which we should, for this reason, develop more than the others, it is not because this dignity is intrinsic to them; it is not because nature itself has, from all eternity, assigned this eminent rank to them; but it is because they have a higher value for the society. Also, as the scale of these values necessarily changes with the society, this hierarchy has never remained the same at two different moments in history. Yesterday it was courage that was in the foreground, with all the faculties that military virtue implies; today it is thought and reflection; tomorrow it will perhaps be elegance of taste, sensitivity to artistic matters. Thus, in the present as in the past, our pedagogical ideal is in every detail the work of society. It is society that draws for us the portrait of the kind of man we should be, and in this portrait all the peculiarities of its organization come to be reflected.

II

In sum, education, far from having as its unique or principal object the individual and his interests, is above all the means by which society perpetually recreates the conditions of its very existence. Can society survive only if there exists

among its members a sufficient homogeneity? Education perpetuates and reinforces this homogeneity by fixing in advance, in the mind of the child, the essential similarities that
collective life presupposes. But, on the other hand, without
a certain diversity, would all co-operation be impossible?
Education assures the persistence of this necessary diversity
by becoming itself diversified and by specializing. It consists, then, in one or another of its aspects, of a systematic
socialization of the young generation. In each of us, it may
be said, there exist two beings which, while inseparable
except by abstraction, remain distinct. One is made up of
all the mental states which apply only to ourselves and to
the events of our personal lives. This is what might be called
the individual being. The other is a system of ideas, sentiments, and practices which express in us, not our personality, but the group or different groups of which we are part;
these are religious beliefs, moral beliefs and practices, national or occupational traditions, collective opinions of every
kind. Their totality forms the social being. To constitute this
being in each of us is the end of education.

It is here, moreover, that are best shown the importance
of its role and the fruitfulness of its influence. Indeed, not
only is this social being not given, fully formed, in the
primitive constitution of man, but it has not resulted from
it through a spontaneous development. Spontaneously, man
was not inclined to submit to a political authority, to respect
a moral discipline, to dedicate himself, to be self-sacrificing.
There was nothing in our congenital nature that predisposed us to become servants of divinities, symbolic emblems
of the society, to render them worship, to deprive ourselves
in order to do them honor. It is society itself which, to the
degree that it is firmly established, has drawn from within
itself those great moral forces before which man has felt his

124

inferiority. Now, if one leaves aside the vague and indefinite tendencies which can be attributed to heredity, the child, on entering into life, brings to it only his nature as an individual. Society finds itself, so to speak, with each new generation, faced with a *tabula rasa*, very nearly, on which it must build anew. To the egoistic and asocial being that has just been born it must, as rapidly as possible, add another, capable of leading a social and moral life. Such is the work of education, and you can readily see its great importance. It is not limited to developing the individual organism in the direction indicated by nature, to eliciting the hidden potentialities which need only be manifested. It creates in man a new man, and this man is made up of all the best in us, of all that gives value and dignity to life. This creative quality is, moreover, a special prerogative of human education. Anything else is what animals receive, if one can apply this name to the progressive training to which they are subjected by their parents. It can, indeed, foster the development of certain instincts that lie dormant in the animal; but such training does not initiate it into a new life. It facilitates the play of natural functions; but it creates nothing. Taught by its mother, the young animal learns more quickly how to fly or build its nest; but it learns almost nothing from its parents that it would not have been able to discover through its own individual experience. This is because animals either do not live under social conditions, or form rather simple societies which function through instinctive mechanisms that each individual carries within himself, fully formed, from birth. Education, then, can add nothing essential to nature, since the latter is adequate for everything, for the life of the group as well as that of the individual. By contrast, among men the aptitudes of every kind that social life presupposes are much too complex to be able to be contained, somehow, in our tissues, to take the form of organic predispositions. It follows that they cannot be transmitted from one generation to another by way of heredity. It is through education that the transmission is effected.

A ceremony found in many societies clearly demonstrates this distinctive feature of human education and shows, too, that man was aware of it very early. It is the initiation ceremony. It takes place when education is completed; generally, too, it brings to a close a last period in which the elders conclude the instruction of the young man by revealing to him the most fundamental beliefs and the most sacred rites of the tribe. Once this is accomplished, the person who has undergone it takes his place in the society; he leaves the women, among whom he had passed his whole childhood; henceforth, his place is among the warriors; at the same time, he becomes conscious of his sex, all the rights and duties of which he assumes from then on. He has become a man and a citizen. Now, it is a belief universally diffused among all these peoples that the initiate, by the very fact of initiation, has become an entirely new man: he changes his personality, he takes another name, and we know that the name was not then considered as a simple verbal sign, but as an essential element of the person. Initiation was considered as a second birth. The primitive mind conceives of this transformation symbolically, imagining that a spiritual principle, a sort of new soul, has come to be incarnated in the individual. But if we separate from this belief the mythical forms in which it is enveloped, do we not find under the symbol this idea, obscurely glimpsed, that education has had the effect of creating a new being in man? It is the social being.

However, it will be said, if one can indeed conceive that the distinctively moral qualities, because they impose privations on the individual, because they inhibit his natural impulses, can be developed in us only under an outside influence, are there not others which every man wishes to acquire and seeks spontaneously? Such are the divers qualities of the intelligence which allow him better to adapt his behavior to the nature of things. Such, too, are the physical qualities and everything that contributes to the vigor and health of the organism. For the former, at least, it seems that education, in developing them, may only assist the development of nature itself, only lead the individual to a state of relative perfection toward which he tends by himself, although he attains it more rapidly thanks to the co-operation of society.

But what demonstrates, despite appearances, that here as elsewhere education answers above all to external, that is social, necessities, is that there are societies in which these qualities have not been cultivated at all, and that in every case they have been understood very differently in different societies. The advantages of a solid intellectual culture have been far from recognized by all peoples. Science and the critical mind, that we rate so high today, were for a long time held in suspicion. Do we not know a great doctrine which proclaims happy the poor in spirit? And we must guard against believing that this indifference to knowledge had been artificially imposed on men in violation of their nature. By themselves, they had then no desire for science, quite simply because the societies of which they were part did not at all feel the need of it. To be able to live they needed, above all, strong and respected traditions. Now, tradition does not arouse, but tends rather to preclude, thought and reflection. It is not otherwise with respect to physical qualities. Where the state of the social milieu inclines the public conscience toward asceticism, physical education will be spontaneously relegated to the background. Something of this sort took place in the schools of the Middle Ages. Similarly, following currents of opinion, this same education will be understood very differently. In Sparta its main object was to harden the limbs to fatigue; in Athens it was a means of making bodies beautiful to the sight; in the time of chivalry it was required to form agile and supple warriors; today it no longer has any but a hygienic end, and is concerned above all with limiting the dangerous effects of a too intense intellectual culture. Thus, even those qualities which appear at first glance so spontaneously desirable, the individual seeks only when society invites him to, and he seeks them in the fashion that it prescribes for him.

You see to what degree psychology by itself is an inadequate resource for the pedagogue. Not only, as I showed you at the start, is it society that outlines for the individual the ideal which he should realize through education, but more, in the individual nature there are no determinate tendencies, no defined states which are like a first aspiration to this ideal, which can be regarded as its internal and anticipated form. There is no doubt that there exist in us very general aptitudes without which it would evidently be unrealizable. If man can learn to sacrifice himself, it is because he is not incapable of sacrifice; if he has been able to submit himself to the discipline of science, it is because it was not unsuitable to him. Through the very fact that we are an integral part of the universe, we care about something else than ourselves; there is in us, therefore, a primary impersonality which prepares for disinterestedness. Similarly, by the fact that we think, we have a certain tendency to know. But between these vague and confused predispositions (mixed, besides, with all kinds of contrary predispositions) and the very definite and very particular form that they take under the influence of society, there is an abyss. It is impossible for even the most penetrating analysis to perceive in advance, in these indistinct potentialities, what they are to become once the collectivity has acted upon them. For the latter is not limited to giving them a form that was lacking in them; it adds something to them. It adds to them its own energy, and by that very fact it transforms them and draws from them effects which had not been contained in them in primitive form. Thus, even though the individual mind would no longer have any mystery for us, even though psychology would be a real science, it would not teach the educator about the end that he should pursue. Sociology alone can either help us to understand it, by relating it to the social conditions on which it depends and which it expresses, or help us to discover it when the public conscience, disturbed and uncertain, no longer knows what it should be.

III

But if the role of sociology is predominant in the determination of the ends that education should follow, does it have the same importance with respect to the choice of means?

Here psychology clearly comes into its own. If the pedagogic ideal expresses, above all, social necessities, they can, however, be realized only in and by individuals. In order that it may be more than just a mental construct, an idle injunction of the society to its members, it is necessary to find the way to make the conscience of the child conform to it. Now, the conscience has its own laws which one must know to be able to modify it, if at least one wishes to be spared the empirical gropings which it is precisely the object of pedagogy to reduce to a minimum. To be able to stimulate activity to develop in a given direction, one must also know what its causes are and what their nature is; for it is on this condition that it will be possible to exert the appropriate influence, based on knowledge. Is it a matter, for example, of arousing either patriotism or the sense of humanity? We shall know all the better how to shape the moral sensibility of our pupils in one or the other direction, when we shall have more complete and more precise notions about the totality of phenomena that are called tendencies, habits, desires, emotions, etc., of the divers conditions on which they depend, of the form that they take in the child. According to whether one sees in such tendencies a product of agreeable or disagreeable experiences that the species has been able to have, or indeed, on the contrary, a primitive fact prior to the affective states which accompany their functioning, one will have to treat them in very different ways in order to regulate their development. Now it is up to psychology, and more specifically, child psychology, to resolve these questions. If it is incompetent to fix the end, or rather the ends, of education, there is no doubt that it has a useful role to play in the establishment of methods. And since no method can be applied in the same fashion to different children, it is psychology, too, that should help us to cope with the diversity of intelligence and character. We know, unfortunately, that we are still far from the time when it will truly be in a condition to satisfy this desideratum.

There could be no question, then, of not recognizing the services which the science of the individual can render to pedagogy, and we shall acknowledge its role. But even in that circle of problems in which it can usefully enlighten the pedagogue, it cannot do without the co-operation of sociology.

First, because the ends of education are social, the means by which these ends can be attained must necessarily have the same character. And indeed, among all the pedagogical institutions there is perhaps not one which is not analogous to a social institution the principal traits of which it reproduces, in a smaller and abridged form. There is a discipline in the school as in the community. The rules which set his duties for the schoolboy are comparable to those which prescribe his conduct for the adult man. The rewards and punishments that are attached to the first are not unlike the rewards and punishments that sanction the second. Do we teach children science ready-made? But the science that is growing teaches itself, too. It does not remain enclosed in the brains of those who conceive it, but it becomes truly operative only on the condition of being communicated to other men. Now, this communication, which sets in motion a whole network of social mechanisms, constitutes an instruction which, in order to address itself to the adult, does not differ in nature from that which the pupil receives from his teacher. Is it not said, besides, that the scientists are teachers for their peers, and is the name of schools not given to the groups that are formed around them? One could multiply examples. This is why, indeed, as the scholastic life is only the germ of social life, as the latter is only the consequence and the blossoming of the former, it is impossible for the principal procedures by which the one operates not to be found in the other. One can foresee, then, what sociology, the science of social institutions, contributes to our understanding of what pedagogical institutions are or to our conjectures on what they should be. The better we understand society, the better shall we be able to account for all that happens in that social microcosm that the school is. On the contrary, you see with what prudence and within

131

what limits it is appropriate to use the data of psychology, even with respect to the determination of methods. By itself alone, it could not provide us with the necessary elements for the construction of a technique which, by definition, has its prototype not in the individual, but in the collectivity.

Moreover, the social conditions on which pedagogical ends depend do not limit their influence to this. They also affect the conception of methods; for the nature of the end implies, in part, that of the means. When society, for example, is oriented in an individualistic direction, all the educational procedures which can have the effect of doing violence to the individual, of ignoring his inner spontaneity, will seem intolerable and will be disapproved. By contrast, when, under pressure of lasting or transitory circumstances, it feels the need of imposing on everyone a more rigorous conformity, everything that can provoke excessive initiative of the intelligence will be proscribed. In fact, every time that the system of educational methods has been profoundly transformed, it has been under the influence of one of those great social currents the effect of which has made itself felt throughout the entire collective life. It is not as a consequence of psychological discoveries that the Renaissance opposed a whole set of new methods to those that the Middle Ages had practiced. But it is because, as a result of the changes that had come about in the structure of European societies, a new conception of man and of his place in the world had emerged. In like manner, the pedagogues who, at the end of the eighteenth century or at the beginning of the nineteenth, undertook to substitute the inductive method for the abstract method, were above all the reflection of the aspirations of their time. Neither Basedow, nor Pestalozzi, nor Froebel were very good psychologists. What their theory expresses above all is that respect for inner liberty, that horror for any restriction, that love of man and consequently of the child, which are at the base of our modern individualism.

Thus, under whatever aspect one considers education, it appears to us everywhere with the same character. Whether it is a matter of the ends that it follows or the means that it employs, it is social needs that it answers; it is collective ideas and sentiments that it expresses. No doubt, the individual himself finds some benefit in it. Have we not expressly recognized that we owe to education the best in us? But this is because the best in us is of social origin. It is always to the study of society, then, that we must return; it is only there that the pedagogue can find the principles of his speculation. Psychology will indeed be able to indicate to him what is the best way to proceed in order to apply these principles to the child, once they are stated; but it will hardly help us to discover them.

I add, in closing, that if there was ever a time and a country in which the sociological point of view was indicated, in a particularly urgent fashion, for pedagogues, it is certainly our country and our time. When a society finds itself in a state of relative stability, of temporary equilibrium, as, for example, French society in the seventeenth century; when, consequently, a system of education is established which, while it lasts, is not contested by anyone, the only pressing questions which are put are questions of application. No serious doubt arises either over the end to attain or over the general orientation of methods; there can, then, be controversy only over the best way to put them into practice, and these are difficulties which psychology can settle. I do not have to tell you that this intellectual and moral security is not of our century; this is at the same time its trouble and its greatness. The profound transformations which contemporary societies have undergone or which they are in process of undergoing, necessitate corresponding transformations in the national education. But although we may be well aware that changes are necessary, we do not know what they should be. Whatever may be the private convictions of individuals or factions, public opinion remains undecided and anxious. The pedagogical problem is, then, posed for us with greater urgency than it was for the men of the seventeenth century. It is no longer a matter of putting verified ideas into practice, but of finding ideas to guide us. How to discover them if we do not go back to the very source of educational life, that is to say, to society? It is society that must be examined; it is society's needs that must be known, since it is society's needs that must be satisfied. To be content with looking inside ourselves would be to turn our attention away from the very reality that we must attain; this would make it impossible for us to understand anything about the forces which influence the world around us and ourselves with it. I do not believe that I am following a mere prejudice or yielding to an immoderate love for a science which I have cultivated all my life, in saying that never was a sociological approach more necessary for the educator. It is not because sociology can give us ready-made procedures which we need only use. Are there, in any case, any of this sort? But it can do more and it can do better. It can give us what we need most urgently; I mean to say a body of guiding ideas that may be the core of our practice and that sustain it, that give a meaning to our action, and that attach us to it; which is the necessary condition for this action to be fruitful.

CHAPTER IV

THE EVOLUTION AND THE ROLE OF SECONDARY EDUCATION IN FRANCE*

(1) My role, gentlemen, is not to teach you the technique of your profession; it can be learned only through practice, and it is through practice that you will learn it next year.** But a technique, whatever it may be, quickly degenerates into a vulgar empiricism if the one who uses it has never thought about the end that it pursues and the means that it employs. To turn your thinking to matters of education and to teach you to apply it systematically to them, is precisely what my task will be. Indeed, pedagogical instruction should propose, not to communicate to the future practitioner a certain number of procedures and formulae, but to give him full awareness of his function.

---

* This introductory lecture had been preceded by a first meeting at which Rector Liard, M. Lavisse, M. Langlois, director of the pedagogical museum, had apprised the students of measures taken to organize their professional training. The address of M. Langlois appeared in the *Blue Review* for November 25, 1905.

** During their second year of training, the candidates for the *agrégation* do a course of practice teaching in the *lycées* of Paris.

But precisely because this instruction necessarily has a theoretical character, certain people doubt that it can be useful. It is not that one would go so far as to maintain that routine can suffice and that tradition has no need to be guided by an advised and informed reflection. At a time when, in all spheres of human activity, one sees science, theory, speculation, that is to say, in sum, reflection, penetrating practice more and more and enlightening it, it would be too strange that only the activity of the educator should be an exception. No doubt, one can criticize severely the use which too many pedagogues have made of their reason; one can legitimately find that their systems, so artificial, so abstract, so little related to reality, are without great practical utility. However, this is not a sufficient motive for proscribing pedagogical reflection forever and declaring it without reason for being; and one readily recognizes, indeed, that this conclusion would be unwarranted. Only one thinks that because of his status, the teacher in the *lycée* has no need to be specially trained and practiced in this particular form of reflection. Such training, of course, is needed by the teachers in our primary schools! Because of the more limited culture that they have received, it may be necessary to stimulate them to meditate on their profession, to explain to them the reasons for the methods that they employ, so that they may use them with discernment. But with a teacher in secondary education, whose mind, first at the *lycée* and then at the university, has been made keen in every way, trained up to all the high disciplines, all these precautions are only a waste of time. Let him be put before his pupils, and immediately the power of reflection that he has acquired in the course of his studies will be applied naturally to his class, even though it would not have been submitted to any preliminary education.

There is, however, a fact which hardly appears to attest

to this native aptitude for professional reflection that is attributed to the *lycée* teacher. In all forms of human behavior into which reflection is introduced, we see, to the degree that reflection is so developed, that tradition becomes more malleable and more amenable to innovations. Reflection in fact is the natural antagonist, the born enemy of routine. It alone can prevent habits from being caught in an immutable, rigid form, which prevents them from changing; it alone can keep them adaptable, maintain them in the state of necessary adaptability and flexibility in order that they may vary, evolve, adapt to the diversity and the changes of circumstances and milieux. Conversely, the less is the part of reflection, the greater is that of resistance to change. Now, it is found that secondary education is remarkable, not for an immoderate appetite for innovations, but for a veritable abhorrence of the new. We shall see how in France, although everything has changed, although the political, economic, moral regime has been transformed, there has been something, however, that has remained relatively unchangeable: these are the pedagogical conceptions which are at the base of what may be called classical education. Except for some superficial additions, the men of my generation were still pupils under an ideal which did not differ appreciably from that by which the schools of the Jesuits in the time of the Great King were inspired. There is truly nothing there which allows us to think that the spirit of criticism and of inquiry had played a role of any significance in our scholastic life.

This is because it is not true that one is qualified to reflect on a given order of facts merely because one has the occasion to exercise his reflection in a different order of phenomena. Many are the great scientists who have made outstanding contributions to their science, but who, however, with respect to everything outside their specialty, are as children. These bold innovators behave in other contexts as simple persons acting by routine, who neither think nor act otherwise than the ignorant populace. The reason for this is that the prejudices which hinder the play of reflection differ according to the order of things to which they apply; it can be, then, that the same mind may be free on one point, while on another it remains in servitude. I knew a very great historian, whose memory I revere and respect, and who, in the matter of education, had remained, or very nearly, with the ideal of Rollin. Besides, each category of facts has to be reflected upon in its own way, according to methods which are appropriate to it; and these methods are not improvised, but must be learned. It is not enough, then, to have reflected upon the beauties of dead languages, or on the laws of mathematics, or on either ancient or modern history, in order to be *ipso facto* in a position, and to have an aptitude, for reflecting methodically on educational matters. But this particular form of reflection constitutes a specialty which calls for a preliminary initiation; the rest of this lecture will be the proof of this.

(2) Not only does nothing justify the privilege that is thus meant to be conferred on the secondary school teachers; not only do we not see why it would be useless to arouse pedagogical reflection in them by an appropriate culture, but, in certain respects, it is more indispensable to them than to others.

In the first place, secondary education is far more complex than primary education. Now, the more complex an entity is, the more complex its life is, the more does it need reflection in order to be able to operate. In an elementary school, each class, at least in principle, is in the hands of only one teacher; consequently, the instruction that he gives

138

has a unity that is quite natural and very simple; it is the
very unity of the person who is teaching. As he oversees the
entire instruction, it is relatively easy for him to determine
the place of each discipline, to adjust them to one another,
and to make them all co-operate toward the same end. But
it is quite different at the *lycée*, where the various courses,
attended at the same time by the same pupil, are generally
given by different teachers. There is here a true division of
pedagogical labor, and one which increases daily, furthermore, modifying the former pattern of our *lycées* and rais-
ing a serious question with which we shall have to be concerned some day. By what miracle could unity result from
this diversity? How would these courses be able to be
reconciled with one another, to be completed in such a way
as to form a whole, if those who give them do not have the
feeling of this whole and of the manner in which each must
co-operate in it. Although we may not at present be in a
position to define the end of secondary education—a question which will be able to arise usefully only at the end of
the course—still, we can say that at the *lycée* it is not a matter of making either a mathematician, or a man of letters,
or a naturalist, or an historian, but of shaping a mind by
means of letters, history, mathematics, etc. But how will
each teacher be able to discharge his function, the part
which is assigned to him in the total work, if he does not
know what this work is, how his various collaborators co-
operate in it with him, in such a way that his efforts fit into
theirs?

Very often, it is true, one reasons as if all that took care
of itself, as if this common end were not at all obscure, as if
everyone knew what it is to form a mind. But in reality this
vague formula is empty of any positive content; and that is
why I was just able to use it without at all prejudicing the

results which our ultimate researches will give. All that it declares is that minds must not be specialized; but this principle does not teach us on what model they must be formed. The manner in which minds were shaped in the seventeenth century would not be suitable today; minds are formed in the primary school too, but otherwise than at the *lycée*. So long, then, as teachers will have only such imprecise adages as a guide, it is inevitable that their efforts should be scattered, and paralyzed as a result of this dispersion.

And it is too often this spectacle which education in our *lycées* presents. Here each one teaches his specialty as if it were an end in itself, although it is only a means to an end to which it should always be related. At the time when I was teaching in the *lycées*, a Minister, to fight against this anarchical atomization, instituted monthly meetings to which all the teachers of a given establishment were to come to discuss questions of common concern to them. Alas, these meetings were never more than empty formalities! We went to them with deference, but we were able to state very quickly that we had nothing to say to one another, because we lacked any common objective. How could it be otherwise so long as, at the University, each group of students receives its chosen instruction in a kind of watertight compartment? The only way to prevent this state of division is to bring all these collaborators of tomorrow to meet together and to think collectively about their common task. At a given moment in their training they must be put in a position to take notice, in its entire scope, of the scholastic system in the life of which they will be called upon to participate; they must see what makes for its unity, that is to say, what ideal its function is to realize, and how all the parts that make it up should co-operate in this final end. Now, this initiation can be accomplished only by means of a course of instruction the plan and method of which I shall presently determine.

(3) But there is more. Secondary education today is found in very special conditions which make such instruction exceptionally urgent. Since the second half of the eighteenth century it has been going through a very grave crisis which has not yet reached its end. Everyone recognizes that it cannot remain what it was in the past; but we do not see with the same clarity what it is to become. Hence these reforms which, for almost a century, follow in order periodically, attesting at the same time to the difficulty and urgency of the problem. To be sure, one could not, without injustice, fail to recognize the importance of the results obtained: the old system was opened to new ideas; a new system is being formed, which appears full of youthful enthusiasm. But is it too much to say that this new system is still trying to find itself, that it is still not sure of itself, and that the former system was tempered by fortunate concessions much more than it was changed? One fact makes particularly apparent the confusion in our ideas on this point. In all previous periods of our history, one could define in a word the ideal that educators proposed to realize in the children. In the Middle Ages the master of the Faculty of Arts wanted above all to make *dialecticians* of his students. After the Renaissance the Jesuits and the directors of our university colleges adopted the end of forming *humanists*. Today we lack any expression to characterize the objective that education in our *lycées* should pursue; this is because we see only rather confusedly what this objective should be.

And let no one think that the difficulty can be resolved by saying that our duty is quite simply to make men of our students! This solution is completely verbal; for it is precisely a matter of knowing what idea we should form of man, we Europeans, or still more specifically, we Frenchmen of the twentieth century. Each people has, at each moment of its history, its own conception of man; the Middle

Ages had its own, the Renaissance had its own, and the question is to know what ours should be. This question, besides, is not peculiar to our country. There is no great European State in which it is not posed, and in almost identical terms. Everywhere, pedagogues and statesmen are aware that the changes that have come about in the material and moral organization of contemporary societies necessitate parallel and no less profound transformations in this particular part of our scholastic system. Why is it especially in secondary education that the crisis rages with such intensity? This is a question which we shall have to examine one day; for the moment, I limit myself to stating the fact, which is not debatable.

Now, to emerge from this era of trouble and uncertainty, one could not count only on the efficacy of decrees and regulations. Whatever their authority may be, decrees and regulations are never more than words which can become realities only with the co-operation of those who are charged with applying them. If, then, you whose function it is to make them live, if you accept them only reluctantly, if you submit to them without believing in them, they remain a dead letter and without useful results; and according to the manner in which you will interpret them, they will be able to produce quite different or even opposite effects. These are hardly more than plans the final outcome of which will depend always on you and on your attitudes. How important it is, therefore, to put you in a position to form an enlightened opinion! As long as men's minds will be full of indecision, there is no administrative decree that can put an end to it. One does not decree the ideal; it must be understood, liked, desired by all those who have the duty of realizing it. It is necessary, in a word, that the great work of reconstruction and reorganization which is indicated be the work of the same body which is called upon to reconstruct and reorganize itself. It must be provided, then, with all the means necessary for it to be able to be aware of itself, of what it is, of the causes that impel it to change, of what it should want to become. One understands readily that, to obtain such a result, it is not enough to train future teachers in the practice of their profession; above all, it is necessary to produce in them an energetic effort of reflection, which they should pursue throughout their careers, but which must begin here at the University; for only here will they find the elements of information without which their reflections on the subject will be only ideological constructions and fruitless dreams.

And it is on this condition that it will be possible to revive, without any artificial process, the rather feeble life of our secondary education. For—it cannot be dissimulated—as a result of the intellectual disorder in which it is found, uncertain between a past that is dying and a future yet undetermined, secondary education no longer manifests the same vitality or the same zest for life as formerly. This remark can be made freely about it, for it implies no criticism addressed to persons; the fact which it states is the product of impersonal causes. On the one hand, the old enthusiasm for classical letters, the faith that they inspired, are irremediably shaken. To be sure, there could be no question of forgetting the glorious past of humanism, the services which it has rendered and still continues to render; however, it is difficult to escape the impression that it has partly outlived itself. But, on the other hand, no new faith has yet come to replace that which has disappeared. The result is that the teacher often asks himself, uneasily, what end he is serving and where his efforts tend; he does not see clearly how his functions are related to the vital functions of society.

143

Hence comes a certain tendency to scepticism, a sort of dis-
enchantment, a veritable moral uneasiness, in a word, which
cannot develop without danger. A teaching body without
pedagogical faith is a body without a soul. Your first duty
and your first concern are, then, to restore a soul to the body
into which you are to enter; and you alone can do it. To be
sure, to put you in the condition to fulfill this task, a course
of a few months will not be enough. It will be up to you to
work at it all your lives. But it is necessary, however, to
begin by awakening in you the will to undertake it and by
placing in your hands the most necessary means for you to
do it. Such is the object of the course that I begin today.

(4) You now know the end that I should like to pursue
jointly with you. I should like to put before you the problem
of secondary education as a whole, and that for two reasons:
first, in order that you may be able to form an opinion on
what this culture should become; then, in order that, from
this inquiry made in common, there may emerge a common
sentiment to facilitate your co-operation of tomorrow. And
now, the end having been stated, let us look for the method
by which it can be attained.

A scholastic system, whatever it may be, is formed of
two kinds of elements. There is, on the one hand, a whole
set of definite and stable arrangements, of established
methods, in a word, of institutions; for there are pedagogical
institutions, as there are juridical, religious or political institutions. But at the same time, within the mechanism so
constituted, there are ideas which make it work and which
make it change. Except, perhaps, for rare moments when a
system is at its peak or is stationary, there is always, even
in the most stable and best-defined system, a movement
toward something other than what exists, a tendency toward

an ideal more or less clearly glimpsed. Seen from the outside, secondary education appears to us as a series of institutions the material and moral organization of which is settled; but, on the other hand, this same organization contains in it aspirations which are trying to find expression. Under this fixed, stable life there is a life in motion which, although more hidden, is not at all negligible. Under the past which continues there is always something new which is in process of becoming. With respect to these two aspects of the scholastic reality, what shall our attitude be?

In the first, pedagogues are ordinarily not interested. The divers arrangements that the past has bequeathed to us are of little concern to them; the problem, as they see it, exempts them from attaching any importance to it. Eminently revolutionary spirits, at least for the most part, present reality is without interest for them; they tolerate it only impatiently and dream of freeing themselves from it, to build from the ground up an entirely new scholastic system in which the ideal to which they aspire is adequately realized. Hence what do they care about the practices, the methods, the institutions that existed before them? It is on the future that they have their eyes fixed, and they believe that they can evoke it from nothing.

But we know today how chimerical and even dangerous are these enthusiasms of iconoclasts. It is neither possible nor desirable that the present organization collapse in an instant; you will have to live in it and make it live. But for that, you must know it. And it is necessary to know it, too, in order to be able to change it. For these creations *ex nihilo* are quite as impossible in the social order as in the physical order. The future is not improvised; one can build it only with the materials that we have from the past. Our most fruitful innovations consist very often of casting new ideas

145

in the old molds, which it is sufficient to modify partially in order to adapt them to their new content. Too, the best means of realizing a new pedagogical ideal is to use the established organization with only slight modification, if necessary, to shape it to the new ends which it is to serve. How many reforms there are which can be accomplished easily, without its being necessary to change existing curricula drastically! It suffices to know how to use profitably those which are in force, by animating them with a new spirit. But to be able so to use the pedagogical institutions that exist, one must not ignore their present makeup. One acts efficaciously on things only to the degree that one knows their nature. One can guide well the evolution of a scholastic system only if one begins by knowing what it is, of what it is made up, what the conceptions are that are at its base, the needs which it answers, the causes that have created it. And thus a whole study, scientific and objective, but the practical consequences of which are not difficult to perceive, appears as indispensable.

It is true that, usually, this study does not seem bound to be very complex. As a long practice has familiarized us with the facts of scholastic life, they seem quite simple to us, and of a nature such as to raise no question that calls for an elaborate series of investigations to be resolved. For many years we have known, under the name of secondary, an education intermediate between the primary school and the University; we have always seen schools around us and classes in the schools, and consequently we are led to believe that all these arrangements take care of themselves, and that there is no need to study them at length in order to know where they come from and what needs they serve. But as soon as one considers things historically instead of regarding them in the present, the illusion is dispelled. This

146

scholastic hierarchy with three levels did not exist at all times, even among us; it dates from yesterday. Until quite recent times secondary education was indistinct from higher education; today the break in continuity which separates it from primary education tends to be wiped out. The schools, with their system of classes, do not go back beyond the sixteenth century, and we shall see that in the revolutionary period there was a time when this system disappeared. Not by far do they correspond to a sort of eternal necessity! And this is because these institutions are not tied up with the universal needs of man at a given level of civilization, but with definite causes, with very particular social conditions which only historical analysis can disclose to us. Now, it is only to the extent that we shall have arrived at determining them, that we shall truly know what this education is. For to know what it is, is not simply to know its external and superficial form; it is to know what its significance is, what place it has, what role it plays in the whole of the national life.

Let us beware, then, of thinking that a little understanding and culture are enough to resolve easily such questions as these: What is secondary education? What is a school? What is a class? We can, indeed, by a mental analysis, abstract rather easily the notion that we personally form of one or another of these realities. But of what advantage can this quite subjective conception be? What we must succeed in discovering is the objective nature of secondary education, the currents of ideas from which it has resulted, the social needs which have called it into existence. Now, to know them, it is not enough to consider them among ourselves; since it is in the past that they have produced their effects, it is in the past that we must see them operating. Far from taking for granted the conception of them that we carry in us, we must, on the contrary, hold it suspect; for, as the product of our limited individual experience, the function of our personal temperament, it can be only partial and delusive. It is necessary to start afresh, to raise systematic doubts, and to treat this scholastic world which is to be explored as an unknown land in which there are real discoveries to make.

The same method is indicated for all problems, even the most specialized, which the organization of education can raise. Whence comes our system of competition (for it is really too simple to impute the whole responsibility for it to the Jesuits)? Whence comes our system of discipline (for we know that it has varied in time)? Whence come our principal scholastic practices? These are questions the existence of which one hardly suspects as long as one remains enclosed in the present, and the complexity of which appears only when one studies them in history. We shall see, for example, how the place which the exegesis of texts, both ancient and modern, has come to occupy and continues to occupy, in our classes, has to do with one of the essential traits of our mentality and of our civilization; and it is in studying medieval education that we shall be led to make this proposition.

(5) But it is not enough to know and to understand our scholastic machinery as it is presently organized. Since it is called upon to evolve continuously, it is necessary to be able to appreciate the tendencies to change which operate on it; it is necessary to be able to decide, knowing what we are about, what it should be in the future. To settle this second part of the problem, is the historical and comparative method equally indispensable?

It may at first glance appear superfluous. Is not the

Evolution and Role of Secondary Education

ultimate object of every pedagogical reform to see to it that the students may be more men of their time? Now, to know what a man of our time should be, what can the study of the past, it is said, teach us? It is neither from the Middle Ages, nor from the Renaissance, nor from the seventeenth or eighteenth centuries that we shall borrow the human model that the education of today should have as its end to realize. It is the men of today who must be considered; it is we ourselves who must be taken into consideration; and it is above all the model of the man of tomorrow which we must try to perceive and to abstract from ourselves.

But at the outset, it is far from easy to know what the exigencies of the present time are. The needs experienced by a great society such as ours are infinitely manifold and complex, and even keen observation of ourselves and our surroundings would not suffice to let us discover them in their entirety. From the narrow milieu in which each of us is placed, we can perceive only those which touch us very closely, those which our temperament and our education best prepare us to understand. As for the others, seeing them only from afar and confusedly, we have only weak impressions of them, and we are led, therefore, not to pay any attention to them. Are we men of action, do we live in a business milieu? We are inclined to make practical men of our children. Do we like speculation? We extol the benefits of scientific culture, etc. When, therefore, one practices this method, one is bound to end up with one-sided and particularistic conceptions which are mutually contradictory. If we want to avoid this particularism, if we want to form a little more complete notion of our time, we must go out of ourselves, we must broaden our point of view and undertake a whole set of researches in order to get at those diverse aspirations which the society feels. Fortunately, even though

149

they may not be very strong, they come to be overtly expressed in a form which renders them observable. They are embodied in those reform projects, those reconstruction plans that they inspire. It is to these projects that we must go to get at them. This, notably, is how those doctrines built by the pedagogues can serve us. They are instructive, not as theories, but as historical facts. Each pedagogical school corresponds to one of those currents of opinion which we are so interested in knowing and reveals it to us. A whole study is thus needed, the object of which will be to compare them, to classify them and to interpret them.

But it is not enough to know these currents. We must be able to appreciate them; we must be able to decide if there is reason to accept them or to reject them, and, in the case where it is appropriate to incorporate them into practice, in what form. Now, it is clear that we shall not be in a position to estimate their value merely by knowing them in their most recent form of expression. One can judge them only in relation to real, objective needs which have produced them and to the causes which have given rise to these needs. According to what the causes will be, according to whether or not we shall have reasons to believe them bound up with the normal evolution of our society, we shall have to accept or reject them. It is these causes that we must get at. But how can we arrive at them, if not by reconstructing the history of these currents, by going back to their origins, by seeking in what manner and as a function of what factors they have developed? Thus, in order to be able to anticipate what the present must become, just as much as to be able to understand it, we must get out of it and turn back to the past. You shall see, for example, how, in order to account for the tendency that leads us today to set up a different scholastic type from the classic type, we shall have to go back beyond recent controversies, to the eighteenth and even to the seventeenth century. And already the very fact of establishing that this movement of ideas has lasted for almost two centuries, that, since the time when it appeared, it has always gained more force, will demonstrate its necessity better than all the dialectic controversies in the world could do.

Furthermore, in order to be able to envisage the future with a minimum of risks, it is not enough to open one's mind to reforming tendencies and to be systematically aware of them. For, despite the illusions which reformers too often foster, it is not possible for the ideal of tomorrow to be entirely original; there will enter into it, certainly, much of our ideal of yesterday, which it is therefore important to know. Our mentality is not going to change completely overnight; we must, then, know what it has been in history, and, among the causes that have contributed to forming it, which are those that continue to operate. It is all the more necessary to proceed with this caution, because a new ideal always appears as in a state of natural antagonism to the old ideal which it aspires to replace, although, in fact, it is only its consequence and its development. And in the course of this antagonism, it is always to be feared that the bygone ideal may disappear completely; for new ideas, having the strength and the vitality of youth, readily wipe out the old conceptions. We shall see how a destruction of this kind took place in the Renaissance, at the time when humanistic education was established: of medieval education, there is almost nothing left, and it is very possible that this total abolition has left a serious lack in our national education. It is important that we take all possible precautions in order not to fall again into the same error, and that if, tomorrow, we must end the era of humanism, we may know how to preserve whatever part of it should be retained.

Thus, from whatever point of view we take, we can know

151

with some assurance the path that remains for us to travel only if we begin by considering carefully what stretches behind us.

(6) You can now understand the significance of the title which I have given to this course. If I intend to study with you the manner in which our secondary education was formed and developed, it is not in order to devote myself to pure researches; it is to arrive at practical results. To be sure, the method which I shall follow will be exclusively scientific; it is that which the historical and social sciences employ. If I was able to speak, just before, of pedagogical faith, it is not because I have the intention of preaching any; I shall remain, here, a man of science. Only, I think that the science of human affairs can serve to guide human behavior usefully. To behave well, says an old adage, one must know oneself well. But we know today that in order to know ourselves well, it is not enough to direct our attention to the superficial portion of our consciousness; for the sentiments, the ideas which come to the surface are not, by far, those which have the most influence on our conduct. What must be reached are the habits, the tendencies which have been established gradually in the course of our past life or which heredity has bequeathed to us; these are the real forces which govern us. Now, they are concealed in the unconscious. We can, then, succeed in discovering them only by reconstructing our personal history and the history of our family. In the same way, in order to be able properly to fulfill our function in a scholastic system, whatever it may be, it must be known, not from the outside, but from within, that is to say, through history. For only history can penetrate under the surface of our present educational system; only history can analyze it; only history can show us of what

elements it is formed, on what conditions each of them depends, how they are interrelated; only history, in a word, can bring us to the long chain of causes and effects of which it is the result.

Such, gentlemen, will be the course that you will be given here. It will be, in the true sense of the word, a pedagogical course, but one which, because of the method employed, will differ markedly from what is usually called by this name, since the works of the pedagogues will be, for us, not models to imitate, not sources of inspiration, but documents on the spirit of the time. I hope that pedagogy, thus reinterpreted, will finally succeed in recovering from the discredit, unjust in part, into which it has fallen; I hope that you will learn how to free yourselves of a prejudice which has lasted too long, that you will understand the interest and the novelty of the enterprise, and that you will, therefore, give me the active co-operation that I ask of you, and without which I could do no useful work.

PEDAGOGICAL REFERENCES

Bain, Alexander (1818-1903)—Scottish philosopher, professor at Aberdeen; works on psychology, philosophy and education. He believed that education should mold both the intellect and the character of the young, and that memory should be strengthened, but physical education should be ignored.

Basedow, Johann Heinrich (1724-1790)—German pedagogue who based his methods on Locke and Comenius; stimulated by Rousseau's *Emile* to reform education, he exercised some influence as a pedagogical writer and agitator. He stressed pleasurable interest in learning, realistic instruction, object teaching, physical education, improved texts, and conversation for teaching foreign languages.

Buisson, Ferdinand (1841-1932)—French educator, reshaped the primary educational system of France; held chair of pedagogy at the Sorbonne, 1896-1902.

Comenius, Johann Amos (1592-1670)—Moravian churchman and educator, pioneered in modern methods of teaching; wrote first picture textbook for children. His realistic approach included education for social life and belief in universal education.

Compayré, Gabriel (1843-1913)—French educator and pedagogue, writer of widely used works on pedagogy.

Descartes, René, (1596-1650)—The pedagogical influence of Descartes was particularly important in the French schools of the latter part of the seventeenth century (cf. Oratory and Port-Royal). He stressed the experimental approach (anti-Aristotelian), urging the reconstruction of educational theory.

Epicurus (341-270 B.C.)—The Epicurean philosophy of pleasure as the goal of life, of happiness as the criterion of behavior, appears in the pedagogical thinking of Rabelais, Montaigne, and Rousseau.

Erasmus, Desiderius (1466-1536)—This Dutch scholar formulated the humanistic ideal of education: the awakening of intelligence, consideration of the capacity of the pupil, developing critical insight, and educating through nature, practice and training, by qualified teachers.

Fontenelle, Bernard L. de (1657-1757)—French philosopher of progress; emphasized reason as the means by which truth can be ascertained.

Froebel, Friedrich (1782-1852)—German pedagogue who, applying the ideas of Pestalozzi, established the first kindergarten, to develop the personality of the child in a balanced fashion.

Guyau, Marie-Jean (1854-1888)—French poet, philosopher and writer on pedagogy who stressed the practical and social point of view in the intellectual, moral and civic training of children.

Hamelin, Octave (1856-1907)—French philosopher and historian of philosophy; taught at the Sorbonne.

Helvetius, Claude-Adrien (1715-1771)—French utilitarian philosopher and littérateur, influenced by Locke. He held that all men are equal, with a natural equality of intelligences, and that any differences among men are attributable to differences in their education.

Herbart, Johann Friedrich (1776-1841)—German philosopher, psychologist, and pedagogue. He emphasized the important role of the student himself in learning and taught that learning takes place through the association of new ideas with already existing ones.

Jacotot, Jean-Joseph (1770-1840)—French educator who developed a method of instruction through constant repetition, questions, and practice. He believed that the will to use intelligence leads to differences among men, all men being equal in intelligence.

Jouvency, Joseph (1643-1719)—French Jesuit and humanist, pedagogue, philologist and historian; published school editions of Latin authors.

Kerschensteiner, Georg Michael (1854-1932)—German mathematician and pedagogue; initiated fundamental reform in popular education.

Pedagogical References

Langlois, Charles-Victor (1863-1929)—French historian, professor at the Sorbonne; wrote history of the Middle Ages.

Lavisse, Ernest (1842-1922)—French historian, professor at the Sorbonne; contributed to study of history and to pedagogy.

Liard, Louis (1846-1917)—Vice-rector of the University of Paris; philosopher. In 1885-1893, he participated in the reorganization of higher education in France.

Montaigne, Michel E. de (1533-1592)—The pedagogical relevance of Montaigne is in his Epicurean morality and in his stress on training judgment rather than memory.

Pestalozzi, Heinrich (1756-1827)—Swiss pedagogue who refined and developed the pedagogical ideas of Rousseau, making the normal and natural development of the child central in the educational process, which he defined as the harmonious development of all human capacities.

Rabelais, François (1490-1553)—Although he did not abandon the humanistic emphasis on books in learning, Rabelais formulated a realist philosophy of education, opposed to scholastic formalism. He influenced Montaigne, Locke and Rousseau in this connection.

Rollin, Charles (1661-1741)—French historian and educator who offered modern ideas for the study of history, urging the replacement of Latin by the vernacular.

Rousseau, Jean-Jacques (1712-1770)—In *Emile*, Rousseau outlined the notion of the spontaneous development of the whole, natural man, revolutionizing established theories of the aims and methods of education.

Spencer, Herbert (1820-1903)—Spencer's contribution to pedagogy lies in his turning attention to the physiological aspect of thinking in connection with learning. For him, the purpose of education was to prepare the individual for complete living.

INDEX

159

Education and Sociology

Index